HOW SUPER COOL TECH WORKS

HOW SUPER COOL TECH WORKS

1

PLAY

Some of the coolest technology is the most fun technology, and this chapter is packed with things that are designed for you to play around with in your free time. Explore how holographic headsets, pens that can draw in mid-air, and wafer-thin television screens work.

≫ Play Room

The HoloLens can transform any scene to suit any activity, such as playing a game. The device detects the shapes of the objects in the area and adds interactive holographic images to them wherever you look.

Different uses

≽ The HoloLens can be used as a communication aid. A holographic video window shows the caller, but the technology also allows that caller to see the world just like you do — and even draw holographic instructions before your eyes.

Communication

≽ The holographic processor is able to turn a 2-D design made on a screen into a 3-D version that can be viewed from all angles. The hologram can then be made real using a 3-D printer.

Visualization

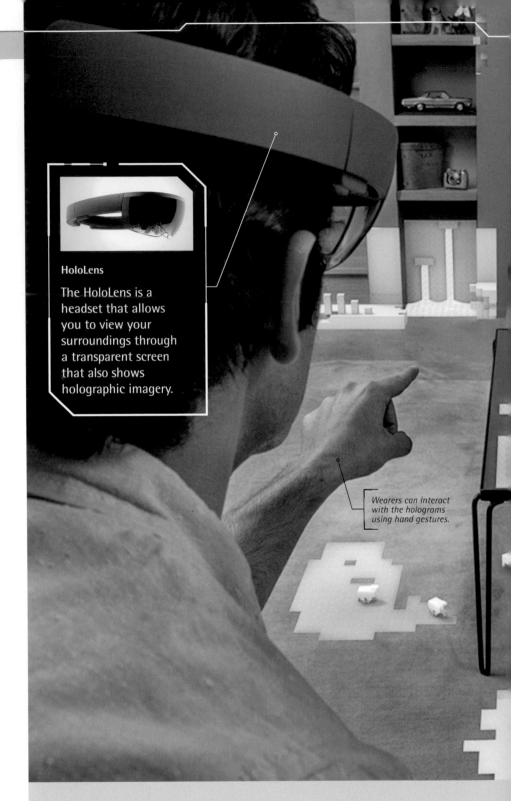

HoloLens

The HoloLens is a headset that allows you to view your surroundings through a transparent screen that also shows holographic imagery.

Wearers can interact with the holograms using hand gestures.

HOLOLENS

The Microsoft HoloLens merges the real and virtual worlds through holographic technology. This is augmented reality, where physical objects have holograms laid over them. The HoloLens can turn any wall into a TV screen, turn any table into a personal computer, or create an entirely imaginary world to explore.

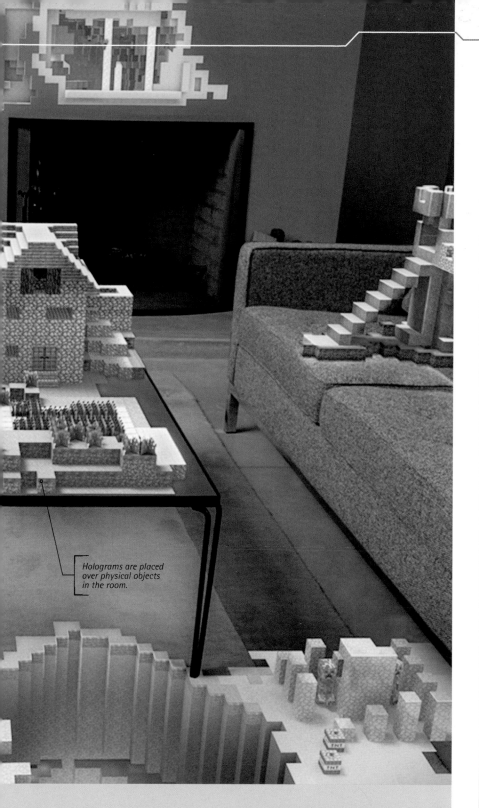

Holograms are placed over physical objects in the room.

HOW IT WORKS

The HoloLens contains three processors: one is the central controller, another is for graphics, while the third scans the surroundings so holograms always appear in the correct places.

« Holograms can be manipulated by swiping, pinching, tapping, and rotating.

» HoloLens can be controlled with a large variety of simple voice commands.

« Sensors in the visor track the user's eyes and adjust the holographic images to match.

» Holograms can be pinned in one place in the scene, so they behave as if they were physical objects.

« Holographic objects can also move around and interact with real objects in the scene.

» HoloLens can also create a scene that is completely filled with computer-generated imagery.

Head-mounted display

Pilots of the F35 Lightning II wear a head-mounted display that receives video feeds from cameras all around the aircraft. Using the display, the pilot can see right through the aircraft – just like wearing a pair of X-ray goggles.

F35 head-mounted display

Cool cameras

Cameras record Baumgartner's historic jump

⌃ In 2012, Felix Baumgartner flew a helium balloon to 38,969 m (127,850 ft) above the deserts of New Mexico, USA — and then jumped out. Action cameras recorded every bit of this incredible journey, from the amazing high-altitude views of Earth to his free fall. The Austrian daredevil broadcast images live to the world as he became the first skydiver to break the sound barrier on his descent, before parachuting safely to the ground.

Large Synoptic Survey Telescope

⌃ The Large Synoptic Survey Telescope is a 3.2-billion-pixel digital camera. Currently being built in the dry mountains of Chile, the device is designed to look for small objects in the Solar System. It will require an array of 1,500 high-definition television screens to display a single full-size picture snapped by the camera.

ACTION CAMERA

Digital cameras have changed the way we record our special memories. Small action cameras are tough enough to be taken anywhere, and also powerful enough to bring back a pin-sharp record of the most exciting action. The high-definition images show what it would be like if you were there, right in the action, doing it yourself.

A sturdy hinged clip pulls the front and back parts of the case together tightly.

Shutter button

Back plate holds LCD screen for playback

Rubber seal makes the case waterproof

Slot for data card

Small front LCD screen shows settings.

Power button is also used for selecting capture modes

GoPro HERO2 camera in protective case

HOW IT WORKS

Much smaller than a phone, the GoPro HERO7 Black is one of the smallest action cameras. In spite of its small stature, the camera is able to capture high resolution images and video, and is waterproof to a depth of 10 m (33 ft).

The camera's power button is on the side.

Video and images from the camera can be synchronized wirelessly to an app.

The camera can be controlled by wireless devices.

The HERO7 Black is the first GoPro camera that can live-stream videos to social media sites.

Smartphone

Tablet

≪ In action

An action camera is often kept in a case to protect it from knocks and water damage. As a result, the camera has few exterior control buttons and is designed to function automatically by remote control or using preset programs.

Shutter operated by sealed plastic piston in case

Plastic case is waterproof to a depth of 40 m (130 ft)

Plastic cover protects lens from scratches

Mount attaches to body, headgear, or sports equipment. It is adjustable so camera can point in the right direction.

Body mounts

This skydiver's view of free fall is taken by a camera mounted on his body. This image was taken by another action camera mounted on a "selfie stick" – a device used to hold the camera further than arm's length.

Skydiving with GoPro

XBOX ONE

The Xbox One is one of the most powerful gaming consoles ever created. Its powerful processors are able to handle detailed and fast-moving graphics across an array of games. It's not just a gaming console, however, as it can also be used as a media centre to stream music and films from the Internet.

An infrared blaster allows the user to control their TV.

Games can be loaded via the disk drive, or downloaded over Wi-Fi.

The 1 TB hard disk stores the operating system and is used to save a player's progress in games.

The power supply unit is at the back of the console.

The Xbox One handheld controller connects to the console wirelessly. It has two control sticks, a directional pad, trigger buttons, and haptic (touch) feedback, which means it vibrates to simulate motions in the game.

Hand-held controller

Console

Xbox One X and controller

The fan keeps the hard-working circuit board cool.

A unique liquid-based cooling system helps to get rid of the heat generated by the powerful processor.

A metal enclosure protects the console's internal parts.

A very powerful processor known as the "Scorpio engine" allows a user to play games at 4K (Ultra HD) resolution while interacting with friends on the "Xbox Live" multiplayer service.

The console's hardware sits inside a slim case.

Great graphics

The Xbox One's graphics are created by a GPU, or Graphics Processing Unit, which is a separate microchip to the main processor. This works with the large internal memory to produce complex, realistic graphics that move smoothly like a video and respond in real time to inputs from controllers.

Graphics from the game Forza Motorsport 6

» Under the hood

The Xbox One X console has much more processing power than a regular desktop or laptop computer, and is able to handle about 6 trillion actions every second. This means it can handle doing multiple things at once – such as playing games and making a video call.

XBOX ONE S

A sleeker, more powerful successor to the original Xbox One, the Xbox One S was the first console to introduce 4K (Ultra HD) resolution gaming.

TABLET
COMPUTER

Without a doubt, the biggest revolution in computing in recent years is the rise of the tablet computer. With the increasing power and decreasing size of computer components, it has been possible to pack a lot of processing power into a small frame. Computers have become smaller, more mobile, and easier to use than traditional desktop or laptop computers. Tablet computers like American company Amazon's Fire HD 10 are designed to be lightweight and portable, yet fast enough to complete everyday computing tasks.

Packs a punch

A powerful processor allows users to easily switch between different tasks, such as watching videos, reading e-books, and playing games.

A large 25.6-cm (10.1-in) HD screen is capable of displaying more than a million colours.

The tablet is 7 mm (0.3 in) thick and weighs about 432 g (15.2 oz).

Tablet layers

The main component of a tablet computer is the large touchscreen, which has to be highly efficient so it doesn't drain the battery. It achieves this by adjusting the number of times the image displayed on screen is updated. When showing videos or games, the display is refreshed 60 times a second, so the eye sees a consistently moving image. However, when the display is of a static subject, the refresh rate is halved, saving valuable energy.

A grid of UV light precisely positions the display's pixels.

A plastic or metal enclosure holds the tablet's components.

The screen has an oil-resistant coating to reduce fingertip smudges.

The battery, processor, and other electronic parts are housed under the screen.

The Kids Edition

The Kids Edition of the Fire HD 10 tablet comes in a robust, protective carry case to protect against damage from accidental drops. A modified user interface allows parents to control their child's online activity, and limit usage to age-appropriate apps, games, and books. The tablet also comes pre-loaded with educational activities designed to engage children between the ages of 3 and 12.

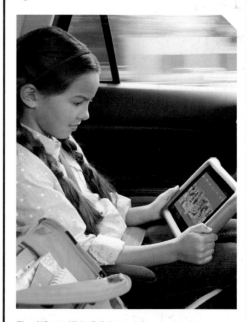

Fire HD 10 Kids Edition with carry case

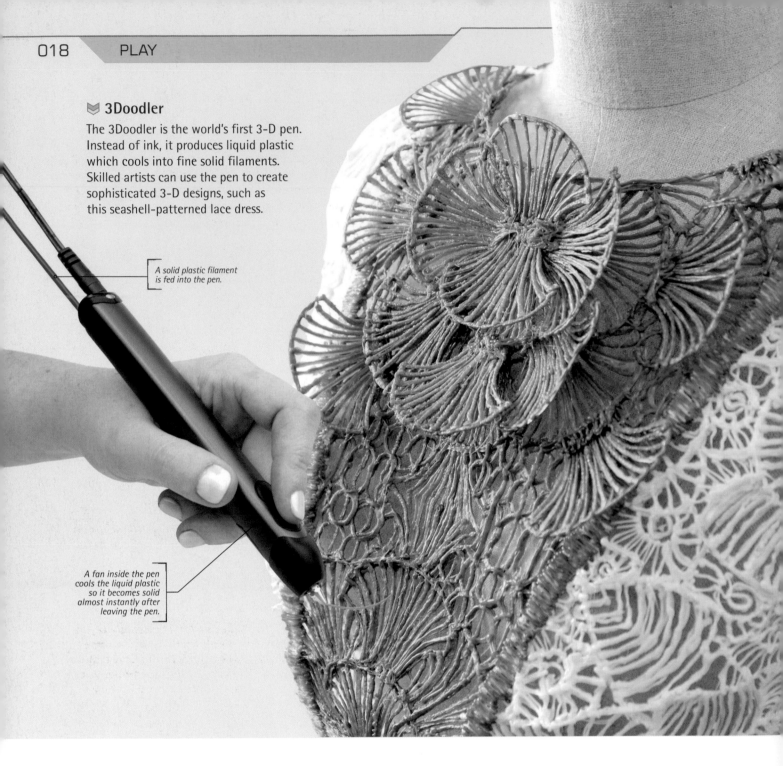

3Doodler

The 3Doodler is the world's first 3-D pen.
Instead of ink, it produces liquid plastic
which cools into fine solid filaments.
Skilled artists can use the pen to create
sophisticated 3-D designs, such as
this seashell-patterned lace dress.

*A solid plastic filament
is fed into the pen.*

*A fan inside the pen
cools the liquid plastic
so it becomes solid
almost instantly after
leaving the pen.*

3-D PEN

Though it may not look like it, the 3Doodler is the smallest 3-D printer
in the world. The basic concept of the 3Doodler is an extension of the
emergence of 3-D printing technology: just as a 3-D printer uses droplets
of quick-drying liquid plastic to produce solid structures, the 3Doodler pen
does the same, but this handheld gadget does it on a smaller scale. Unlike
a normal 3-D printer, however, the pen allows users to develop and change
their designs as they go along.

HOW IT WORKS

A 3-D printer always follows a preset pattern, whereas a 3-D pen is a freehand device entirely controlled by the user. You can use it to create textured artwork on paper, but unlike a regular pen, you can also draw into the air. With practice and patience, a 3-D pen can be used to produce unique models and artworks, and even to draw replacement parts or mend broken components.

Power cable

Coloured plastic filament

Buttons control the speed of the plastic flowing from the pen's tip.

1 A flexible filament of the desired colour is fed into the end of the pen. The filament is thermoplastic, meaning it will become soft and flexible when heated and retain its shape once it cools down.

2 A small heater inside the pen melts the filament, so it becomes a gooey liquid. A pump controlled by buttons on the pen pushes the liquid outwards from the nib.

A double-click produces a continuous flow.

The molten plastic cools to form a solid shape.

Multicoloured objects can be made by using different plastic filaments.

3 The speed at which the plastic flows can be altered to create different effects. Unlike an ink pen, the plastic emerges even when the pen is held still.

4 More complex structures can be constructed from several parts made independently. Once they have cooled sufficiently, these components can be glued together with fresh hot plastic.

Printing food

3-D printers are able to make almost anything you want, and they can make things out of materials other than plastic. The Bocusini system uses food as its material. It can produce intricate dishes from liquid chocolate and dairy products, as well as purees of vegetables and meat.

A marzipan printed cake decoration

TUNING UP

Inspired designers are using revolutionary technology to develop a range of pretty cool new musical instruments. Some of these are based on traditional instruments like violins and pianos. Other technological advances are completely changing the way we play and listen to music.

Seaboard GRAND

ROLI's Seaboard GRAND is a reinvention of the piano. Its soft, touch-sensitive surface gives players more control over sound. They can bend the pitch by moving fingers rapidly from side to side, like vibrato on a violin or guitar, as well as deepen sounds by pressing into the silicone keys.

3Dvarius

The 3Dvarius is a playable electric violin created with a 3-D printer. It is modelled on a famous type of violin made by the Stradivari family in the 17th and 18th centuries. A 3-D printer uses a laser to cure layer after layer of photo-reactive resin, building up the design into a clear plastic violin. Ordinary strings and tuning pegs are attached.

Here Active Listening

Annoying wires trailing from earphones could soon be a thing of the past. Earbuds made by Here Active Listening are completely wireless. They connect to a smartphone app that lets users control volume and filter out unwanted sounds. When not in use, the buds are stored in a case that works as a charger.

Silent Guitar

With Yamaha's Silent Guitar, musicians can play and practise as much as they want without disturbing the neighbours. Plugging in headphones gives the player full sound but the guitar can hardly be heard at all by anyone else. The guitar can be amplified for playing live, and can be dismantled for travelling.

Reactable

The Reactable system is a computer-linked tabletop with an illuminated display of symbols. Users can create music and sound effects by placing objects called tangibles on the table. Different tangibles control different sounds, and interacting with their position on the table changes the sounds the system produces.

Miniaturization

Over the years, scientists and engineers have been able to greatly reduce the size of silicon chips that drive electronic devices. As smart watch screens get bigger, the silicon chips that run them have become thinner than a human hair! Yet these chips have more processing power than ever before – such that we may even see watch-sized personal computers in the future.

Miniature smart watch components

Easy connectivity

The Galaxy Watch Active2 can be paired with the Galaxy Buds earphones using Bluetooth. The Buds then allow the user to easily switch between listening to music, making calls, or following map directions.

Galaxy Buds

The Galaxy Watch Active2 is available in two sizes. This is the smaller version, with a 40-mm (1.5-in) watch face.

WatchPad

The concept of the smart watch has been about for a while. This prototype WatchPad was released by American technology company IBM in 2001. It connected to the Internet, received emails and texts, but had limited functions and a battery life of only a few hours.

⬇ Mix and match

The Galaxy Watch Active2's body is made out of lightweight aluminium, but users also have the option of buying a stainless steel version. It is simple to change the look of the watch by taking the strap off and changing it for another colour.

Watch straps are available in different materials such as leather, silicon, and textile.

Back button

The Galaxy Watch Active2 with the 44-mm (1.7-in) watch face has a larger battery to power its slightly larger screen.

Microphone

Home button

SMART
WATCH

As computer chips get smaller and more powerful, it has become possible for them to drive something as small as a wristwatch. The Galaxy Watch Active2 is an example of a "smart watch". It tells the time, but its computer makes it possible to make and receive calls and messages, and use apps. The watch connects to the phone network and Internet.

PS4

Since its launch in late 2013, tens of millions of the PlayStation 4 (PS4) consoles have been bought by gamers across the world. It has become the most popular gaming console of recent years. Its popularity is largely based on the powerful technology inside its small frame – the PS4 offers the most impressive graphics and speed of any console currently available. Players can connect their smartphones to the console to play games on a mobile device, and a virtual-reality headset was released in 2016.

Inside a PlayStation 4

A metal bracket protects the circuitboard and hard drive underneath.

The hard drive stores games, the operating system, and game save data.

A fan-assisted heatsink under the circuitboard makes sure the electronics do not overheat.

⟫ Under the hood

The PlayStation 4's internal hardware is similar to a home computer, which makes it easier for developers to make games for the console. The PS4 is able to carry out 1.8 trillion separate calculations every second.

The power supply keeps the console running.

The optical drive is used for loading games and playing DVDs and Blu-ray discs.

No Man's Sky

No Man's Sky is a PS4 game that contains an entire, fictional universe. This computer universe is on the same scale as our own, containing 18 quintillion planets – or 18 million trillion. Players explore these planets, collecting resources and discovering what is there, and every planet has unique animals, weather, and landscape. The game designers did not plan each one – there are too many for that. Instead, they set up rules that govern the universe and allow the computer to create each planet as players arrive.

Alien life created in *No Man's Sky*

Console and controller

The PS4 console is supplied with a wireless DualShock controller that connects using Bluetooth. There is also a motion-sensing system that works with the device, using two cameras to capture the position and movements of players and translating this into game play on screen. Players can also log in to the console by allowing the cameras to scan their face.

The console can be positioned horizontally or vertically, using a stand.

DualShock controllers come in a variety of colours.

PS4 and controller

DUALSHOCK

The PS4 DualShock controller has two joysticks, several trigger buttons, and a trackpad. It also contains accelerometers, which detect the motion of the controller so it can be used like a steering wheel. When more than one controller is connected to a console, the light bar on each one illuminates in a different colour, matching the player's character on screen.

Touchpad used for fingertip control

Circuitboard handles the inputs from the buttons and joysticks

Motors in handles create vibration feedback

Light bar on the top of the controller lights up when it is in use

Rechargeable battery

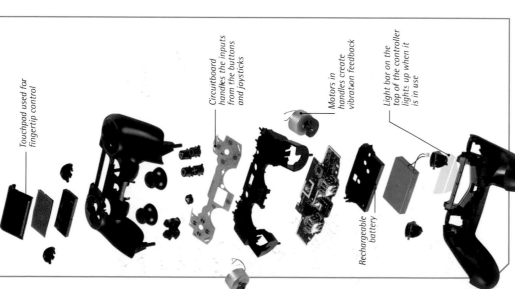

HOW IT WORKS

An OLED display has pixels that are able to make a dot of any colour by mixing red, blue, and green light. Each pixel contains three different OLED molecules that make light of one of these three colours. The quality of colour images is improved because the OLEDs make only the exact colours required, and do not filter them from a white light source like other systems.

1 *Negative cathode sends electrons through OLED*

2 *The emissive layer transports electrons from the cathode to the conductive OLED layer, and makes light.*

3 *Conductive OLED layer connects the cathode to the anode*

4 *The transparent positive anode sits under the screen's surface.*

5 *The screen surface shows the light produced. The colour of the light depends on the chemical make-up of the OLED.*

OLED structure

The display system is the depth of a credit card, and light enough to be hung on the wall like a picture.

≫ Curved screen

This TV produces a high-definition picture from a layer of OLEDs, or light-emitting diodes. That layer is 200 times thinner than a strand of hair, making an OLED screen flexible enough to be curved.

OLED TV

The future of television is here. TV manufacturers have tweaked traditional light-emitting diode (LED) TVs to add an organic (carbon-based) layer that produces coloured light. The key to the technology is its carbon-based organic compound layer – traditional LED screens use several layers to make light and colour, but the new OLED screens use only one. They produce images with better colours that change faster than LEDs. OLED TVs have thinner screens, use less energy, and are less polluting than other TVs.

OLEDs create 16 million colours by combining red, green, and blue light produced by three kinds of chemicals.

Flexi-Tech

The screen of this flexible display contains a layer of OLEDs sandwiched between transparent plastic electrodes. It is flexible enough to bend or twist, and could even be rolled up. Flexible screens like this are being used in curved mobile phones and tablets, where the screen wraps around the edge so messages can be displayed along the side of the device. Flexible OLED displays are even lightweight enough to be stitched on to fabric. As well as displays, OLEDs can produce light of a single colour and be a highly versatile form of low-energy lighting that can be used just about anywhere.

A flexible OLED display

INSTRUMENT 1

The basic designs of musical instruments haven't altered in hundreds of years, but technology is now changing all of that. The Artiphon Instrument 1 is a guitar, piano, violin, and drum machine all in one. It is designed to respond to the gestures a musician uses to play any of these instruments, and it can respond to different pressures for playing loud or soft, fast or slow. It can be played as a live instrument in the normal fashion, or used to record a sound symphony by connecting it to a computer.

Played like a violin   Strummed like a guitar   Played like a cello

≫ Palette of sounds

The Instrument 1 has a pressure-sensitive surface that works on the same principles as a touchscreen or touchpad. It can be plucked, strummed, and tapped to emulate the keys, strings, and bowing action of several traditional instruments.

HOW IT WORKS

The Instrument 1 is played using a touch-sensitive fingerboard and six buttons on the bridge. If set in guitar mode, the bridge buttons are used for plucking and strumming, while touching the fingerboard alters the pitch. In piano mode, the fingerboard becomes a stacked six-octave keyboard, while for drumming, the fingerboard is divided into 12 pads.

Bridge for strumming, picking, or tapping

The fingerboard has ridges that can work as six strings.

An in-built accelerometer detects the orientation of the instrument.

There are loudspeakers at either end.

Volume control and mode selector

Capo buttons are used for changing the key setting on the fingerboard.

The spaces between ridges are used as keys or pads.

A rechargeable battery under the touchpad means it can be played anywhere.

New sounds

⌄ French inventors have created a jelly-making kit that has a special twist: it can be used to make music. The coloured, salty jellies are placed on a capacitor board that stores electrical energy. When you touch a jelly, it changes the electric field of the board, creating a sound that varies according to the shape, colour, and saltiness of the jelly.

Musical jellies

⌄ Some instruments don't even need you to touch them to be able to play. The theremin was invented by Léon Theremin in 1928. It has two "antennas", which produce small electric fields. Moving your hands into a field alters its strength, which changes the sound given out by the machine. Moving closer to the tall antenna makes the note rise in pitch. Moving a hand away from the side antenna makes the sound louder.

Léon Theremin playing the theremin

3-D PRINTER

Traditionally, the process of making physical products was long, expensive, and difficult. It was often hard for designers, engineers, architects, and manufacturers to build, test, and refine their ideas. These days, however, it is possible for all of these professions to turn their ideas into reality by using a 3-D printer. It works just like a regular printer: a set of instructions is sent to the printer from a computer, and the printer turns these into a physical object. The latest 3-D printers can build complex shapes and even objects with moving parts. In future, they might be as inexpensive and as common as 2-D printers are now, making it possible for us to make many of the things we buy today.

HOW IT WORKS

The printer melts a continuous filament of solid material and squeezes the liquid out through a fine nozzle on to a baseplate. The baseplate or the nozzle, or both, move according to a set of instructions to control where the liquid goes. When the first layer has been laid down, another layer is squeezed out on top of it. Then more layers are laid down, one by one, gradually building up the shape of a 3-D object.

A reel of plastic supplies a continuous filament of printing material.

Print head

Filament

Heating coil

Insulated sleeve transfers heat from the coil to the filament

Nozzle

How filament is melted

The object is created by the print head, which can move along all three axes.

The object is built up, layer by layer.

The baseplate supports the object being printed.

A 3-D printer is about the size of a microwave oven.

« Printing in 3-D

This 3-D printer is building up a model of a human skull. 3-D printers can make objects from a variety of materials, including plastic, metal, a stretchy rubber-like material, and even materials that mimic stone or wood.

3-D printing in space

The days when space station astronauts had to wait weeks or months for a tool or a replacement part to be sent up from Earth may be over. A 3-D printer was delivered to the International Space Station (ISS) in November 2014, enabling astronauts to make some of the things they needed. The printer was designed to work in the ISS's weightless environment. A few weeks after it arrived, the crew used it to make a socket-wrench – the instructions for the tool were sent to the ISS printer from Earth, and it took four hours to make.

NASA's 3-D printer for use in space

The shape of a skull is created as the print head moves while it prints.

RFID TAGS

American football is one of the latest sports to embrace radio frequency identification (RFID) technology. RFID tags produce unique short-range radio signals that can identify and track any object or person. As well as being used to track athletes in sporting events, RFID tags are used on many passports, to monitor books loaned out to people and returned to libraries, and on bank and pre-paid travel cards for contactless payments.

Radio frequency identification

These American football players have tiny radio tags in their uniforms. These provide real-time data about their locations and speeds, allowing fans to review and compare the latest performance statistics of their team's players.

Battery-powered tags the size of a coin are fitted inside the player's shoulder pads.

Passive Tags

At 0.7 mm (0.02 in) thick, passive RFID tags are small enough to fit into credit cards and packaging. The tags have no power source, but produce a weak radio signal when activated by a stronger radio wave from a tag-reading device. The tag's tiny ID signal can only be detected over a distance of about 5 cm (2 in).

RFID Chip

HOW IT WORKS

» Each player's tags broadcast ID signals 25 times a second. The signals are powerful enough to reach a loop of 20 radio receivers located around a field's edge.

The tags send out a radio signal unique to each player.

Battery boosts the RFID tag's signal

Receiver

« The receivers pick up signals from all the tags on the field. The further away a tag is from a receiver, the weaker the signal the receiver picks up. This information is used to calculate the exact location of each player.

» The tags track the speed and direction of players at every step of the game. This makes it possible to compare the running speeds of defensive and offensive players as they compete for the ball.

#98   PLAYER
40
30
20
10
0

« The tag data from a game can be used to generate amazingly detailed performance statistics, such as how quickly players are able to change direction, their average jump height, and how often they stop for a rest.

TECH TOYS

Toy designers are constantly coming up with amazing new ways of using advanced technology to create playthings for children. There is now a huge range of high-tech toys that are both fun and educational. They include robots that "know" their owners, Internet-linked toys, and interactive games.

CogniToys Dino

Dino is an Internet-linked dinosaur toy for children aged 5–9 that responds when spoken to. Children ask Dino questions (and get answers), give it commands, and interact with its jokes and stories. As a child gets smarter, so does Dino, matching the child's abilities in rhyming, maths, spelling, and other skills.

Code-a-Pillar

The Code-a-Pillar has eight segments that can slot together in any order, and each segment has an explanatory icon and controls one action, such as going forwards or flashing lights.

Once started, Code-a-Pillar performs a series of tasks in whatever order its segments are connected. By giving children lessons in sequencing, Code-a-Pillar can be seen as a first step in computer coding.

Wondernik

These craft kits set both boys and girls the challenge of making their own toys. Wondernik uses a range of different parts to teach children how things like motors, batteries, and switches work, and how to sew and draw. The kits include talking animals, a nightlight house, and a wearable animal tail.

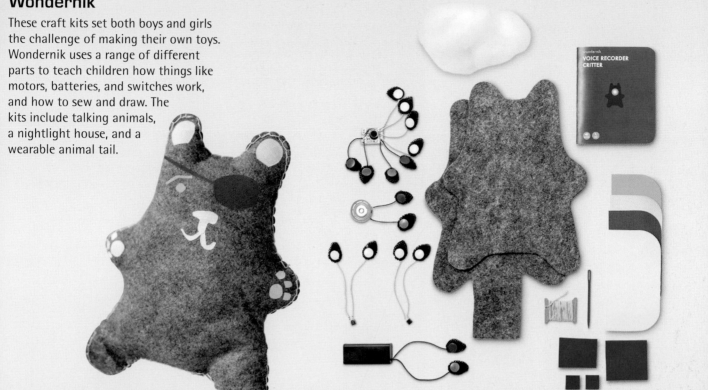

Osmo

Combining physical tiles and an app, and a special scanner that fits over a tablet's front-facing camera, Osmo is a puzzle game with a twist. The app displays a puzzle, and the scanner lights up the tiles when they are put in the right places. Osmo comes with five games, including spelling, drawing, and number puzzles.

Portable powerhouse

❧ The screen can be adjusted as on a normal laptop, but it can also be twisted around to face the opposite direction to make a drawing surface.

Adjusting the screen

❧ The laptop is encased in magnesium, a tough but lightweight metal. The whole device weighs about 1.5 kg (3.3 lb) and is about 23-mm (0.9-in) thick when folded shut.

Surface Book from the side

Hinge connectors grip the screen by expanding inside the sockets when electrified.

A stylus pen can be used for drawing and navigation on the screen. It connects to the computer by Bluetooth.

SURFACE BOOK

Able to work as a laptop, a tablet computer, or a touch-sensitive canvas, the Microsoft Surface Book shows how computers are changing to match the way we live and work. This fully portable and highly flexible gadget provides superfast file transfer and a seamless experience in gaming, video editing, moviemaking, 2-D and 3-D rendering, and other graphics-intensive tasks.

The 35-cm (13.5-in) display has 6 million liquid-crystal pixels, backlit by light-emitting diodes (LEDs).

HOW IT WORKS

The touchscreen detects a touch as a disturbance in a tiny electric field that covers its surface. When a finger (or pen) makes contact with the screen, some of the electric charge moves into the finger. To replace the charge lost from that part of the screen, tiny currents flow from power sources in the four corners. The processor in the computer is able to work out where the person is touching as a result.

Finger touching glass cover pulls tiny charge out of electrode

Changes in charge show where finger is touching

A processor scans charge distributed across the electric field and registers it as an action on the screen.

Screen time

» The Surface Book has a liquid-crystal display (LCD), which shows images as coloured dots. Light shines through minute dots called pixels, which each have a red, blue, and green filter. When liquid crystals are electrified, they block light from passing through particular filters in the pixel, creating images.

Liquid-crystal display (LCD)

⌂ Laptop-tablet

The Surface Book is a laptop with a detachable screen that can function separately as a tablet computer. To work as a tablet, the screen houses the memory, storage, processors, and a battery. The keyboard base has an additional battery.

Osborne 1

« Laptops have come a long way since the Osborne 1, which was released in 1981. It weighed nearly 10 times as much as a Surface Book and was four times the price. Its main drawback, however, was its tiny 13 cm² (5 in²) screen.

Sticks of light and colour

Once a glowstick is activated, it glows for as long as the chemical reaction inside it continues, and can't be reactivated afterwards. The longest lasting glowsticks can keep glowing for up to 12 hours.

GLOWSTICKS

Glowsticks are responsible for the forest of brightly coloured lights you often see at parties and pop concerts, but they also have more serious uses. They are often used for emergency lighting on trains and planes. Walkers, climbers, and sailors also carry them to signal to rescuers at night if they get into trouble. Glowsticks are popular light sources because they are inexpensive, they can be stored for long periods, and they can be activated quickly without any need for batteries or other power supplies.

HOW IT WORKS

Glowsticks do not glow if they are not activated. To use one, you need to bend it, which breaks the small, brittle tube of hydrogen peroxide inside it. The outer tube is flexible and so does not break. When the hydrogen peroxide reacts with a chemical compound called diphenyl oxalate, energy is released. This is absorbed by a dye, which gives out the energy as coloured light, with different dyes producing different colours.

1 *This glowstick is inactive.*

Glass vial containing hydrogen peroxide

2 *The vial of hydrogen peroxide is broken.*

3 *The hydrogen peroxide mixes with the other chemicals.*

Flexible plastic casing

4 *A chemical reaction releases coloured light.*

Bioluminescence

Various organisms, like the jellyfish shown here, can make parts of their body glow by using chemical reactions similar to those used in glowsticks. The effect is called bioluminescence. Insects such as fireflies and glow-worms use bioluminescence to attract mates or warn predators to stay clear. Some deep-sea fish have glowing lures that look like small creatures to attract prey.

Bioluminescent jellyfish

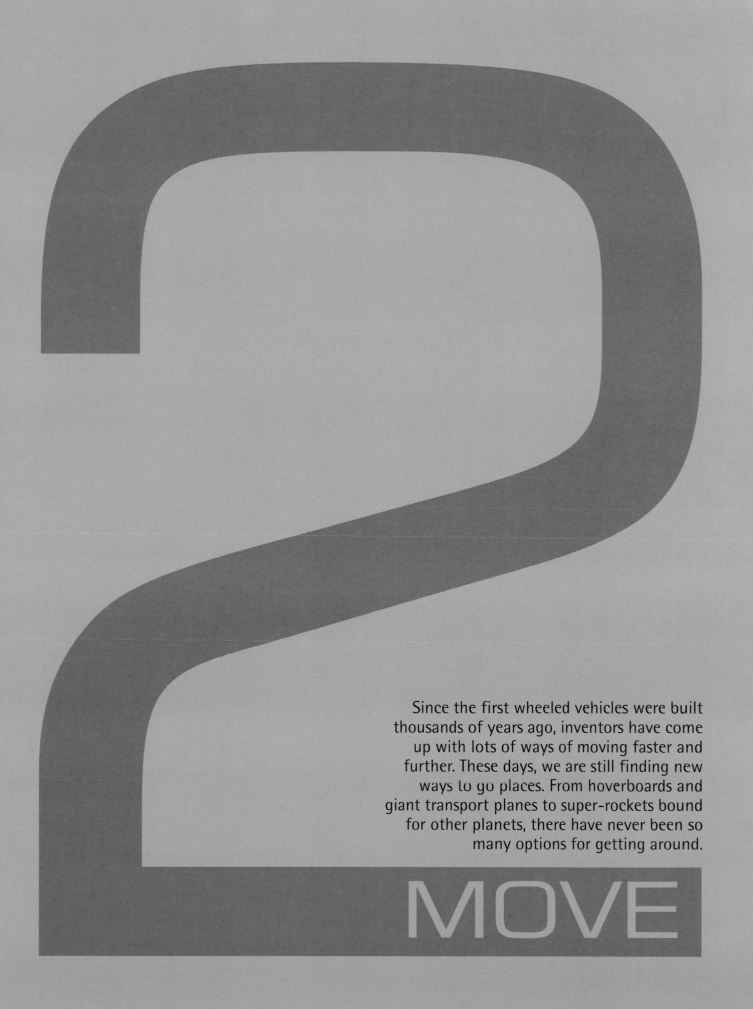

Since the first wheeled vehicles were built thousands of years ago, inventors have come up with lots of ways of moving faster and further. These days, we are still finding new ways to go places. From hoverboards and giant transport planes to super-rockets bound for other planets, there have never been so many options for getting around.

MOVE

HOVERBOARD

The hoverboard used to be pure science fiction. But in 2015, the Lexus Slide was unveiled in a one-of-a-kind "hoverpark" in Barcelona, Spain. The Slide makes use of the principle of magnetic levitation, and it took 18 months of research and development to make it so it was small and light enough to fit inside a skateboard.

The magnets in the base of the board are superconductors. To work, they have to be kept at −192°C (−314°F) by using liquid nitrogen.

Supercooled nitrogen creates a fog

⟫ No wheels

The Lexus Slide hoverboard is a unique piece of equipment. The wheel-less board can flip, ollie, and grind like a normal skateboard, but it never touches the ground. The Slide is a one-of-a-kind project designed by the Japanese car company Lexus.

HOW IT WORKS

The Slide has a total of 32 supercooled superconductors hidden in its thick base. The magnetic forces from the track under the ground turn these conductors into powerful magnets, which push back with an equal force. The result is that the board and its rider are lifted off the ground. The board holds enough liquid nitrogen to levitate for 10 minutes before needing a refill.

Slide is 92 cm (36 in) long and weighs 11 kg (24 lb).

Two containers of liquid nitrogen under the wooden deck cool the superconductors.

Magnetic field

The track is built from permanent magnets.

Gliding on water

The Slide is pushed forwards by the rider's kicks, like a normal board, but is locked to the magnetism of the hoverpark's hidden track, gliding wherever that leads – even over water.

Hoverboard on a water-covered track

Shanghai Maglev Train

Shanghai Maglev Train

The same principles of magnetic levitation used by the Slide are put to use in maglev trains, such as the Shanghai Maglev Train (SMT). As it floats frictionless above the ground, the train is pushed along at high speeds by a wave of magnetic forces running through the track.

Display showing the train's speed

The SMT is the world's fastest passenger train. It makes the 30-km (18.6-mile) journey from Shanghai's central station to the airport in 7.3 minutes. Its maximum speed of 431 kph (268 mph) is faster than that of a Formula 1 race car.

SUPER ROCKET

Falcon Heavy is the world's most powerful rocket. Built by American company SpaceX, it is designed to launch payloads (satellites or spacecraft) weighing up to 53 tonnes into space. When a Falcon Heavy rocket blasts off, its engines produce almost as much thrust as 18 jumbo jets, which is essential as the rocket needs to reach a speed of 40,000 kph (25,000 mph) to break free of Earth's gravity. Once free of Earth, the Falcon Heavy can be used to send astronauts to the Moon or perhaps to Mars.

Light and strong

The thin walls of the Falcon Heavy's three first-stage cores and second stage are made of aluminium–lithium alloy. The addition of lithium makes the metal lighter and stronger than aluminium alone. The payload exterior is made of a lightweight composite material.

Inside the Falcon Heavy

Each of Falcon Heavy's three cores is a Falcon 9 rocket's first stage. The Falcon 9 is already in service.

The 27 first-stage engines burn a mixture of RP-1 kerosene fuel and liquid oxygen. RP-1 is the same fuel used by jet airliners.

⌂ World's most powerful rocket

Falcon Heavy is a two-stage rocket that stands 70 m (230 ft) tall. The first stage has three parts, or cores, each with nine identical rocket engines, making 27 engines in all. Each core is a Falcon 9, an earlier SpaceX rocket.

A streamlined exterior houses the payload and protects it as the rocket travels through the atmosphere. It opens to release the payload.

The second stage burns the same mixture of RP-1 fuel and liquid oxygen. It can be stopped and restarted to place payloads in different orbits.

Cutting costs

Reusable rockets are set to become more common because they cut mission costs. An American company called Blue Origin is developing a wholly reusable rocket. In November 2015 the company successfully brought one of its rockets down to a controlled landing after a sub-orbital test flight.

Rocket capsule and booster

HOW IT WORKS

Most rockets are used only once, and break up as they fall back to Earth. Falcon Heavy is designed to be partly reusable. It has three cores that return to Earth and land. Falcon 9 rockets have already tested this landing system. Following several failures, the core of a Falcon 9 landed successfully after launching a satellite in December 2015, and the first Falcon Heavy rocket launched in 2018.

Nose cone separation

2 The second stage separates and fires its rocket engine.

Payload separation

1 After using all of their fuel in the ascent, the two side cores fall away.

Centre core flips over

3 The centre core and side cores re-enter the atmosphere.

Side cores flip over

Centre core

Launch

4 Landing legs deploy, allowing cores to make a soft landing.

Falcon Heavy flight

Scalevo

Most wheelchairs are unable to climb stairs - but the Scalevo can. On level ground, it acts much like a regular wheelchair, but to climb stairs, it extends a pair of tank-like tracks, and goes up at the rate of one step per second.

Scalevo climbing stairs

WHILL's unique front wheels ride easily over bumps, dips, and other small obstacles that get in the way. They also give a good grip on all surfaces, even on loose gravel or snow.

Innovative design

⬇ Stylish performance

Mobility devices are often large, awkward to steer, and rarely great to look at. WHILL's designers want to change this image. Their device combines top performance and ease of use with a streamlined, futuristic design.

WHILL

For the 100 million wheelchair users worldwide, the everyday world can be a hard place to get around. The WHILL personal mobility device is a new advance in technology that could make the many difficulties they face things of the past. This sleek power-chair, which combines a hefty four-wheel drive (4WD) design with all-directional wheels, is designed for precision control on almost any type of terrain.

Key features

≽ The WHILL mobility device can be controlled remotely by a smartphone app. This also lets the user adjust the seat, alter the driving and control settings, and operate a security locking mechanism.

Using the app to control WHILL

HOW IT WORKS

What makes WHILL so different is the design of the two front wheels. These all-directional wheels run forwards smoothly, but can also get WHILL out of a tight corner. When turning space is limited, 24 small rollers around the edge of each wheel can steer WHILL in any direction, even sideways, or spin the chair round on the spot.

» The seat can slide forwards to let the user get into and out of the chair more easily. The positions of the seat back, arms, and footrest are also adjustable to suit users of different heights and mobility.

Adjusts to suit the user

≽ There is a mouse-like drive control on one handrest, and a switch for adjusting speed on the other. WHILL can travel up to 19 km (12 miles) on a single battery charge and has a top speed of 8.8 kph (5.5 mph).

WHILL's front wheel is made up of 24 small rollers.

Each roller can turn sideways.

Easy-to-reach controls

ELECTRIC CAR

The Tesla Model S looks like many other cars, but it represents an automotive revolution. The Model S is an all-electric car, meaning that instead of having a petrol-guzzling engine, it is powered by an electric motor. It's no slouch, either. It can get from 0 to 100 kph (60 mph) in as little as three seconds and reach a top speed of 250 kph (155 mph). As the Model S doesn't burn any fuel, it doesn't give out any of the harmful greenhouse gases and sooty particles that pollute the environment, doing its bit to lessen our dependence on fossil fuels.

HOW IT WORKS

The Tesla Model S has an advanced electric powertrain that is simpler, lighter, and more efficient than the equivalent system in a conventional car. When the driver presses the accelerator pedal, more electric current flows to the motor that turns the wheels. The motor is also used to slow the car by a process called regenerative braking. This converts the car's kinetic (movement) energy into electrical energy, which is stored in the battery. Most of the car's other functions are controlled via a 43-cm (17-in) tablet-like touchscreen.

Charging port is located at left tail light.

Touchscreen panel is used to control car settings.

Rear-wheel engine

Battery and heavy motor lower the centre of gravity and improve stability.

The lithium-ion battery forms the car's floor. A battery swapping station can replace it with a new one in just 90 seconds.

The Tesla comes in two-or-fourwheel-drive varieties, with the electric motors fitted between the wheels, causing them to turn.

Clever Car

The Model S's sleek body is packed with smart systems. It can steer itself to stay within a lane, change lanes when you tap the turn signal, set its speed by reading road signs, park itself automatically, and brake or steer itself to avoid collisions.

Car components

Front trunk

⌃ The empty engine bay at the front of the car and the absence of a fuel tank at the back provide extra storage space. This increases the total storage space of the car by almost 20 per cent, and makes the car easier to handle as there is less weight in the front of the car.

Plugging in to recharge

⌃ The car's battery can be recharged from any electrical outlet. The charging port opens automatically when the car detects someone approaching with the charging connector. Special chargers are available that can charge half of the battery in 20 minutes.

A passenger on a test flight
floats weightlessly inside
SpaceShipTwo.

HOW IT WORKS

A SpaceShipTwo flight lasts about two and a half hours. A jet aircraft, WhiteKnightTwo, takes off carrying *SpaceShipTwo*. SpaceShipTwo falls away from the jet at 15,000 m (50,000 ft). It fires its rocket and climbs to 110 km (68 miles), crossing the boundary between Earth's atmosphere and space, where passengers experience weightlessness. After six minutes, it begins its descent, and at 24 km (15 miles) above Earth it prepares for landing.

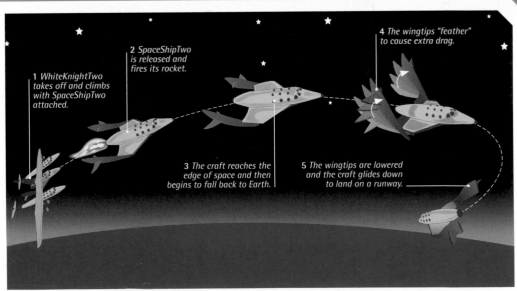

1 *WhiteKnightTwo takes off and climbs with SpaceShipTwo attached.*

2 *SpaceShipTwo is released and fires its rocket.*

3 *The craft reaches the edge of space and then begins to fall back to Earth.*

4 *The wingtips "feather" to cause extra drag.*

5 *The wingtips are lowered and the craft glides down to land on a runway.*

SpaceShipTwo's passengers can enjoy experiencing up to six minutes of weightlessness. They will be allowed to leave their seats and float about their cabin before strapping in again for re-entry to Earth's atmosphere and landing.

Space tourism

SpaceShipTwo is still waiting to carry day trippers but space tourism is already here. The first space tourist was American millionaire Dennis Tito. In 2001, he paid $20 million to spend 7 days, 22 hours, and 4 minutes on board the International Space Station (ISS). He orbited Earth 128 times during his time in space.

Dennis Tito

SPACESHIPTWO

Within a few years, regular citizens could be experiencing the zero-gravity conditions of space on board a specially designed aeroplane called SpaceShipTwo. This rocket-powered craft is designed to carry fare-paying passengers about 100 km (62 miles) into Earth's atmosphere, where space begins, and return them within three hours.

The craft can reach the top speed of 4,000 kph (2,500 mph) that's necessary to break the bonds of Earth's gravity. If the craft's testing continues to be successful, there are plans for a fleet of five spaceplanes to be operated by Virgin Galactic from the purpose-built Spaceport America, in New Mexico, USA.

Alternative energy sources

⌄ One new source of oil fuel can be made with light. Tiny, plant-like algae use a source of bright light to grow inside an algal bioreactor, where they are kept free of impurities. The oils stored in the algae's cells are then refined into a fuel.

A bioreactor grows oil-rich algae

⌄ The dustbins of Copenhagen, Denmark, have become a source of power since the Amager Resource Centre (ARC) opened. This giant incinerator makes electricity from the heat of burning rubbish. The vast building's sloping roof also doubles as a ski run!

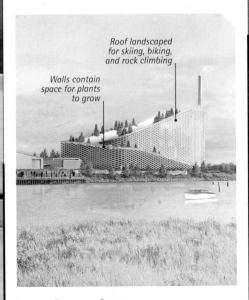

Roof landscaped for skiing, biking, and rock climbing

Walls contain space for plants to grow

Amager Resource Centre

BIO-BUS

Unlike an ordinary bus, the Bio-Bus has an unusual power supply – human poo. Human waste from sewers can be collected and turned into biomethane, a highly flammable fuel. The raw ingredients of biomethane are both plentiful and completely renewable, so the Bio-Bus shows us that clean fuel made in this way could one day be used to power our cars, heat our homes, and generate electricity.

⌄ **Powered by waste**

The Bio-Bus runs a regular public transport service through Bristol, UK, powered by human sewage and food waste. After being processed at a biogas plant, these rotting materials become a super-clean, odour-free, and low-carbon fuel.

This GENeco Bio-Bus

HOW IT WORKS

Biomethane is made by heating waste inside tanks where all the air has been removed. Inside, bacteria turn the poo into biogas, which is 60 per cent methane. Dust, bugs, and bad smells are filtered and the biogas is then refined so it is 98 per cent methane, which can be used as fuel for vehicles, or even supplied to homes.

Sewage works

Home

Waste from homes

12–18 days + 32–42°C (90–108°F)

Bacteria turn poo into biogas

Biogas mixture is rich in methane

Some biogas is used to heat the sewage works

Fuel is ready to be used

Bus

Quality checked before use

Final product is 98% methane, 2% nitrogen

Biogas is filtered

The gas fuel is stored in a streamlined tank on the roof, compressed to 200 times the air pressure in the atmosphere.

...wered by your waste for a sustainable future   GENeco   Sustainable Solutions

Tell us what you think #biobus

The 40-seater bus can travel 300 km (186 miles) on a full tank of biogas.

The exhaust emissions contain 97 per cent less smoke and 90 per cent less nitrogen oxide than diesel-powered buses.

HOW IT WORKS

ElliptiGO foot platforms and drive arms are designed to produce the same smooth elliptical foot motion as an elliptical trainer. There are various models, with different stride lengths and stride heights to suit different users. A workout on an ElliptiGO uses the same muscles as running, but without the impact of feet pounding the ground, so it's equally suitable for leisure riders, athletes recovering from injuries, and ageing riders with aching joints.

⇗ The rider starts by pushing down with one foot and forwards with the other.

⇗ The foot platforms move drive arms that turn the main gearwheel.

⇗ The main gearwheel turns the rear wheel via a drive chain. An experienced rider can reach speeds of 30 kph (20 mph) or more.

ELLIPTIGO

The ElliptiGO combines running and cycling in a unique machine. It's the brainchild of Bryan Pate, an American former athlete who was unable to run after suffering hip and knee injuries. Cycling is gentler on the joints than running, but can lead to neck and back pain. By combining the two in the ElliptiGO, users burn 33 per cent more calories, but avoid many of the potential stresses and strains of either exercise.

⟫ Standing room only

ElliptiGO combines an elliptical trainer, or cross-trainer, with a bicycle. Instead of sitting down and turning pedals, as on a normal bike, the rider stands up and uses a running action, as if using an elliptical trainer in a gym.

Riding an ElliptiGO in a standing position burns 33 per cent more calories than riding a conventional bike.

The rider stands on large platforms that support the rider's weight.

The higher riding position makes it easier for the rider to see and be seen by other road users.

Bizarre bikes

Bikes have been made of all sorts of material, including cardboard and even grass. The cardboard bike is glued together and treated to make it waterproof and fireproof. The grass bike is made from a famously strong type of bamboo. These bikes are becoming more popular because they are inexpensive and environment-friendly.

Cardboard bike

The handlebars are higher than on a normal bike to suit the rider's standing position.

ELLIPTIGO

➤➤ Multipurpose crew vehicle

Four astronauts in full launch suits test out the Orion's control array in a prototype crew module. NASA is developing Orion to carry human crews, first to the International Space Station, then to the Moon, and possibly even to Mars.

Space Launch System

A new launch rocket is being developed to carry Orion into space. Known as the Space Launch System (SLS), it will be the most powerful rocket ever built, capable of lifting at least 70 tonnes – the weight of 13 African elephants – into orbit. The main rocket will have four engines of the same design used by the Space Shuttle. Two solid-fuelled rocket boosters will add to the thrust. The first SLS launch is planned for 2020.

SLS flight concept

ORION

The Orion spacecraft is the next step in human space exploration, designed to take crews into deep space for the first time since the last Apollo Moon mission in 1972. The spacecraft draws on engineering developed over the 50-year-long Space Race, and makes use of design concepts from the Apollo project, the Space Shuttle launch system, and life-support technology used on space stations.

HOW IT WORKS

Orion is made up of modules, each of which have specific functions. Four astronauts travel inside the pressurized crew module, while the service module behind holds the main rocket engine and the guidance jets used to steer in space. Both modules are launched on top of a rocket, but when returning to Earth, the crew module breaks off and is the only part that re-enters the atmosphere.

Service module contains fuel and air tanks, plus any cargo

Crew module is 50 per cent larger than the Apollo craft that flew to the Moon

Spacecraft is covered by an aerodynamic cone during liftoff flew to the Moon

Launch exterior breaks away after reaching space

Escape rockets pull the crew module away from the main rocket if there is an emergency

⩘ Heat shield protects crew module during re-entry

⩘ Module parachutes to an ocean splashdown

Orion powered by four solar arrays

HOW IT WORKS

The pilot wears a heat-resistant flight suit similar to a firefighter's gear to protect him from the hot engines and jet exhaust. Fuel stored inside the wing flows to the engines. The engines burn the fuel and generate thrust. The pilot controls the engines with a handheld throttle.

Winglets improve the efficiency of the wing.

Each engine generates 22 kg (50 lb) of thrust.

The wing holds 30 litres (8 gallons) of fuel.

Heat-resistant suit

The throttle varies the engine thrust.

Two jet engines nestle under each side of the wing.

≫ Flying free

Rossy makes flying his jet-powered wing look easy as he speeds through the sky over Dubai, United Arab Emirates. When fully loaded with fuel, his aircraft weighs just 55 kg (121 lbs).

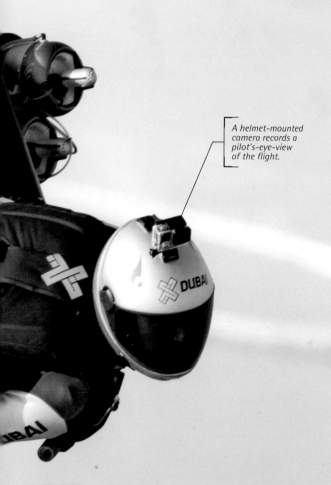

A helmet-mounted camera records a pilot's-eye-view of the flight.

JET WINGS

Swiss pilot Yves Rossy loves flying. In fact, he loves flying so much that he doesn't always bother with a plane. He transforms himself into a jet aircraft by strapping a wing and four jet engines to his back. He has flown over the Alps in Europe and Mount Fuji in Japan, and across the English Channel. Rossy has even flown in formation with the Airbus A380, the world's largest passenger airliner.

Flying high

» The jet-powered wing has to be launched in the air, so Rossy takes off in a plane, helicopter, or hot-air balloon – but his 2-m (6.5-ft) wingspan means he has to hold on to the side as he can't get into the craft. He starts his four jet engines and jumps from the aircraft, often launching himself with a spectacular back-flip. He then fires up the engines and streaks away.

A back-flip launch

» With about 80 per cent throttle, Rossy flies at around 180 kph (110 mph). He adjusts how fast he's going with a small control on his right hand, and manoeuvres by twisting his body or moving his hands. There are two instruments mounted on his chest – an altimeter that shows his altitude and a timer that tells him how much fuel is left.

Jetman in mid-flight

» After almost 10 minutes, with most of his fuel gone, Rossy throttles down the engines and turns them off. He then pulls a handle to open his parachute. With the extra weight of the wing on his back, landing can be tricky. He only tries to land standing up when there is almost no wind. Usually, he has to land parallel to the ground, which can lead to scratches and scrapes.

Descending by parachute

ON THE ROAD

Since the invention of the wheel about 5,500 years ago, inventors and engineers have been searching for better, safer, faster, and easier ways of getting around. From electric bikes and aquatic cars to slick shoes and shape-shifting autos, developers are still coming up with new and exciting ideas.

Copenhagen Wheel

The Copenhagen Wheel is designed to make it easier to pedal a bike, by increasing the power supplied to the wheels. The red wheel hub contains an electric motor and battery. The motor activates when the cyclist pedals, and an app lets you change the level of assistance.

See-through truck

Drivers often find it difficult to get past a lorry safely because the truck blocks the view of the road ahead. One possible solution is to put a camera on the truck's bonnet that sends images to a screen on the truck's back. Drivers behind the truck can then see what's ahead of it, and decide when is safe to overtake.

EO2 Car

Small cars have an advantage when it comes to parking. Few are smaller than the EO2. It's only 2.6 m (8.5 ft) long and it can make itself even smaller. The body tips up at the back and the rear wheels tuck under the body. In addition, all four wheels can swivel 90 degrees, enabling he car to move sideways into tiny parking spaces.

WaterCar

Deep water defeats most cars, but the WaterCar Panther keeps going. The Panther is an amphibious car, equally happy on land or in water. In water, the driver pulls a lever to activate a waterjet at the back of the car, and pushes a button to raise the wheels. The waterjet propels the car. The Panther is fast enough to tow a wakeboarder or waterskier.

Nike FlyEase

Shoes are surely the most basic type of transport invention, but some disabilities make it difficult to tie laces. When 16-year-old American Matthew Walzer, who suffers from cerebral palsy, asked Nike to make a shoe he could put on by himself, they developed FlyEase. Instead of laces, these trainers have a wrap-around zip that can be opened and closed with one hand.

BELUGA AIRBUS

The Airbus A300-600ST (known as the "Beluga") transport plane has been in operation since 1996. This strange-looking super-transporter was developed to carry large parts of aircraft between Airbus-manufacturing and assembly plants in Europe. Airbus maintains a fleet of five Belugas.

VITAL STATISTICS

The Airbus Beluga retains the same basic dimensions as the A300-600 airliner it was developed from. It has a wingspan of 44.8 m (147 ft) and an overall length of 56.2 m (184 ft). The maximum fuselage diameter is 7.1 m (23 ft). The Beluga can carry cargo weighing up to 47 tonnes and as big as the aeroplane's wings. It has carried satellites, helicopters, and even large works of art.

A Beluga before landing

Cargo slides from a loading platform into the plane's gaping cargo hold.

Length

56.2 m (184 ft)

Height

17.2 m (57 ft)

Wingspan

44.8 m (147 ft)

Fuselage

7.1 m (23 ft)

A cavernous cargo hold

The Beluga has one of the biggest cargo holds of any civil or military aircraft in service today. It was built by converting a standard Airbus A300-600 airliner. The top of the fuselage was cut off and a new, bigger fuselage was fitted, giving it a beluga whale shape.

Beluga

The Airbus Beluga was named after the beluga whale. Belugas are not very big compared to other whales. They are only about 6 m (20 ft) long. It was the plane's shape that led to it being named Beluga.

The whale that inspired the name

The front of the cargo hold opens up for loading and unloading.

A larger-than-normal tailfin was fitted to the plane along with small stabilizer fins because the large fuselage changed the airflow around the plane.

HOW IT WORKS

A European project called MUNIN (Maritime Unmanned Navigation through Intelligence in Networks) is developing the technology for operating fully autonomous vessels at sea. The equipment and the control systems are being designed so that they can be fitted to existing as well as new ships.

Robot ship

Satellite

Shore station

1 A ship is monitored by a human from a shore station via a satellite link.

Obstacle

2 The ship can plot a course around an obstacle without human intervention.

3 If required, the shore station can take control from a remote bridge.

Floating resorts

Cruise ships are used to transport passengers between ports of interest, but now the ships are designed as floating holiday resorts. The world's biggest cruise ship, Oasis of the Seas, has a park with living trees, an ice-skating rink, a zip-wire, and a miniature golf course to entertain its 6,000 passengers.

Oasis of the Seas

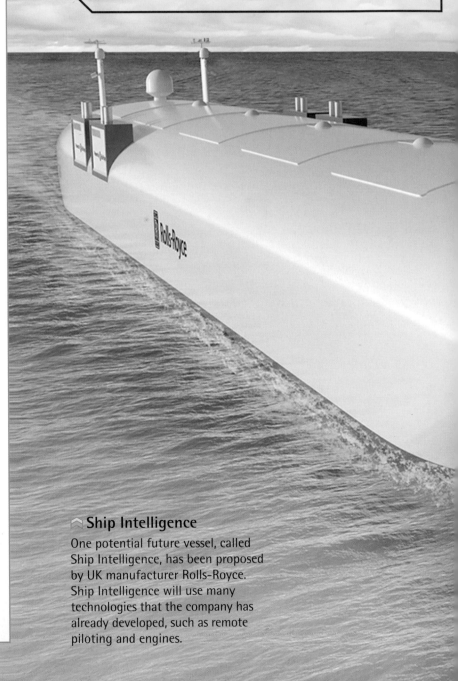

⌃ Ship Intelligence

One potential future vessel, called Ship Intelligence, has been proposed by UK manufacturer Rolls-Royce. Ship Intelligence will use many technologies that the company has already developed, such as remote piloting and engines.

FUTURE
SHIP

In the not-too-distant future, many of the cargo ships that criss-cross oceans may be robot vessels with no crew onboard. They will be safer than crewed ships because 75 per cent of all accidents at sea are caused by human error. If necessary, a crew could take control remotely from a shore-based command centre. The technology and IT systems for these ships are being developed now.

Displays in a virtual bridge

For vessels that require a crew, the ship's bridge will have a total overhaul. The windows will become info-packed augmented reality displays, and will highlight hazards that would be difficult to spot with the naked eye. Smart workstations will recognize crew members as they enter the bridge, and adjust to their personal preferences and settings.

The Solar Wind Around Pluto (SWAP) instrument measures the solar wind, the stream of particles given out by the Sun.

A dish-shaped antenna 2.1 m (6.9 ft) across receives commands from Earth and sends data back.

The crinkly gold covering on the spacecraft is a metal-coated plastic film that regulates the spacecraft's temperature.

Electrical power is generated on board. The heat produced by the decay of radioactive plutonium is harnessed to produce electricity.

NEW HORIZONS

In July 2015, a grand-piano-sized spacecraft took the first close-up images of the small icy world called Pluto at the edge of the Solar System. The spacecraft, New Horizons, had been flying through space for nine years to reach its target.

The amazing quality of the images it beamed back meant the mission had been a total success. The spacecraft carried some of the ashes of American astronomer Clyde Tombaugh, the man who discovered Pluto in 1930.

❰❰ Far from Earth

New Horizons flew within 12,500 km (7,800 miles) of Pluto. The spacecraft was so far away from Earth that radio signals sent from the craft travelling at the speed of light took more than 4 hours to reach its researchers.

Pluto

The images New Horizons captured of Pluto show mountains as big as the Rockies in the US, but Pluto's mountains are made of water-ice. There are also vast plains of ice made of nitrogen, a gas on Earth, but on Pluto it's frozen solid because little of the Sun's light reaches it from 5.9 billion km (3.69 billion miles) away. New Horizons photographed Pluto's five moons. The largest, Charon, is about one-third the size of our Moon.

HOW IT WORKS

Scientists were able to reduce the amount of fuel New Horizons had to carry by using some energy from the giant planet Jupiter as the tiny spacecraft passed it. This type of manoeuvre is called a gravity assist, or a gravitational slingshot. New Horizons gained an extra 14,500 kph (9,000 mph) by harnessing Jupiter's gravitational pull. This boosted the craft's speed to more than 53,540 kph (36,380 mph) and cut its flight time to Pluto by five years.

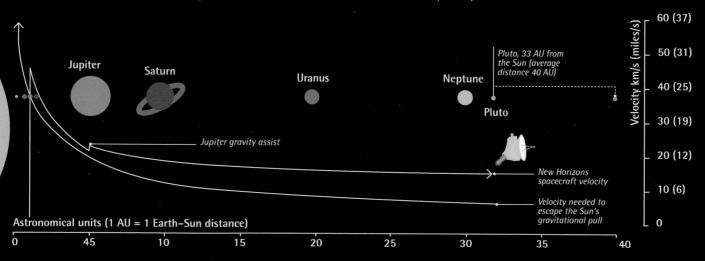

Jupiter

Saturn

Uranus

Neptune

Pluto, 33 AU from the Sun (average distance 40 AU)

Pluto

Jupiter gravity assist

New Horizons spacecraft velocity

Velocity needed to escape the Sun's gravitational pull

Velocity km/s (miles/s)

60 (37)
50 (31)
40 (25)
30 (19)
20 (12)
10 (6)
0

Astronomical units (1 AU = 1 Earth–Sun distance)

0   45   10   15   20   25   30   35   40

HOW IT WORKS

Rotor frame

When lift exceeds the weight of the aircraft, the aircraft takes off.

The rotors generate equal lift across the whole rotor frame.

⌃ For take-off, all of the Volocopter's rotors spin at the same speed, blowing air straight downwards. The downwards force of the rotor blades creates a reaction force according to Newton's Third Law of Motion. The reaction force is lift. This lift raises the craft up.

Changing the rotor speed alters the lift.

The aircraft tilts at the front and flies forwards.

⌃ To fly forwards, the rotors at the back spin faster than those at the front, which generates more lift at the back. The aircraft tilts forwards, directing some of the downdraught from the rotors backwards, which propels the aircraft forwards.

The rotors on one side spin faster.

The aircraft tilts to the side.

The rotor downdraught blows to one side.

⌃ When turning to one side, the rotors on the opposite side to the turn spin faster than the rotors on the turning side, tilting the aircraft so that it is propelled sideways.

VOLOCOPTER

If you've ever been stuck in gridlocked traffic and dreamed of flying over the top of it all, your wish may be about to come true. The Volocopter is a small aircraft designed to be easy to fly. It has seating for the pilot and one passenger. Inspired by the first toy drones that appeared in 2010, a prototype Volocopter made its first flight the following year. Unmanned and also larger passenger-carrying models are on the drawing board, meaning zipping past traffic might not be so far away.

Using the Volocopter

Volocopters could have many uses besides avoiding traffic. With a top speed of 100 kph (60 mph) and an altitude of up to 2,000 m (6,500 ft), they could be used for search and rescue, crop spraying, sports, and as an instrument platform for scientists, surveyors, and film-makers.

Volocopter VC200

⌃ Rotor power

The Volocopter VC200 is lifted into the air by 18 electric rotors fixed to a lightweight carbon frame. More than 100 microprocessors monitor the aircraft and automatically adjust for turbulence. If the pilot lets go of the controls, the craft stays where it is.

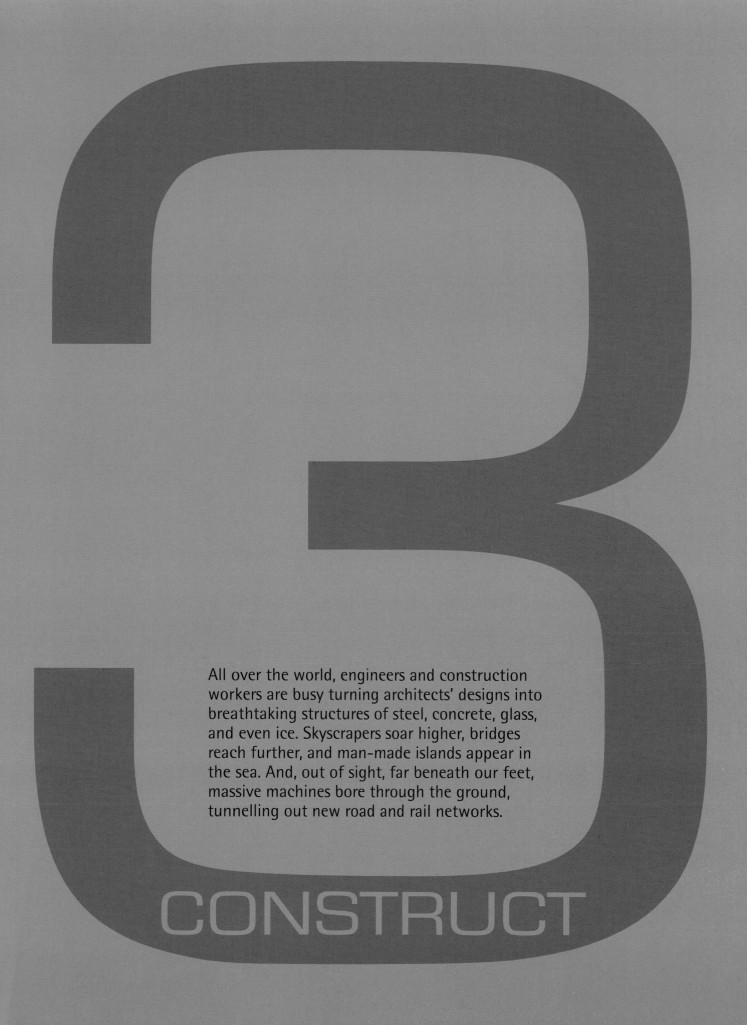

3

All over the world, engineers and construction workers are busy turning architects' designs into breathtaking structures of steel, concrete, glass, and even ice. Skyscrapers soar higher, bridges reach further, and man-made islands appear in the sea. And, out of sight, far beneath our feet, massive machines bore through the ground, tunnelling out new road and rail networks.

CONSTRUCT

SKYSCRAPER

With population levels always rising, creating more places for people to live and work in often means building upwards. Skyscrapers make the most of limited city space by providing thousands of homes and offices high above ground level. The first skyscrapers appeared in Chicago, USA, in the late 19th century. Today, they are a feature of modern cities.

≪ Sky high

The Burj Khalifa in Dubai, United Arab Emirates, is the world's tallest building, at 828 m (2,722 ft). With 200 floors (160 habitable), it contains a mix of residential and office space. It took 22 million man-hours and just under six years to build.

The observation deck on the 148th floor is the highest such platform in the world.

The Burj's aluminium and glass facade can withstand temperatures of more than 45°C (113°F).

There are 57 lifts to carry people and goods 504 m (1,655 ft) up the building.

Coated glass protects the interior of the building from the glare and heat of the Sun.

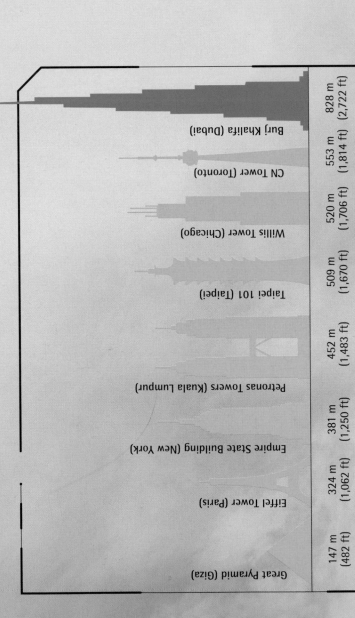

Comparison of heights of iconic world buildings

The Burj Khalifa is twice the height of the Empire State Building in New York, USA. On a clear day, the tip of its antenna can be seen from nearly 100 km (62 miles) away. As a result of its height, it holds other records, too – such as the world's highest restaurant, observation deck, elevator system, and nightclub.

Building	Height
Great Pyramid (Giza)	147 m (482 ft)
Eiffel Tower (Paris)	324 m (1,062 ft)
Empire State Building (New York)	381 m (1,250 ft)
Petronas Towers (Kuala Lumpur)	452 m (1,483 ft)
Taipei 101 (Taipei)	509 m (1,670 ft)
Willis Tower (Chicago)	520 m (1,706 ft)
CN Tower (Toronto)	553 m (1,814 ft)
Burj Khalifa (Dubai)	828 m (2,722 ft)

The Burj's design is inspired by the patterns and styles of Islamic architecture.

The weight of the concrete used in the building equals that of 100,000 elephants.

HOW IT WAS MADE

The Burj rises from the desert

» A special concrete mix was used to ensure that the tower can withstand tremendous weight, as well as high desert temperatures. Three tower cranes lifted concrete up to the 156th level. The structure above this height was created using lighter-weight steel.

« The Burj Khalifa's foundations reach down more than 50 m (164 ft) into the ground. The basic structure used more than 330,000 m³ (11,653,840 ft³) of reinforced concrete. A staggering 33,563 tonnes of steel bars were used to build the tower.

Steel bars from the tower's framework

« A marvel of cutting-edge design and technology, the Burj was officially opened in January 2010. This eagerly anticipated event included a spectacular display featuring light and sound effects, as well as 10,000 fireworks. The megastructure hosts fireworks displays every New Year's Eve.

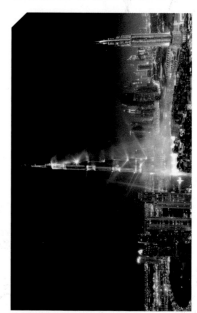

Lights and fireworks mark opening day

BLUE
PLANET

Opened in 2013, the ultra-modern Blue Planet
in Copenhagen is Denmark's national aquarium.
The extraordinary spiral building houses 20,000
creatures in 7 million litres (1.85 million gallons)
of water. Its 53 tanks replicate the conditions
in various watery habitats around the world.

*The tunnel is 2.1 m (6.8 ft)
high and 3 m (9.8 ft) wide,
and is made of acrylic
12 cm (4.7 in) thick.*

*Sharks up to 4 m (13 ft)
long swim around
visitors in the tunnel.*

*A transparent section of the
walkway floor lets visitors
watch sharks and other fish
swimming below their feet.*

HOW IT WORKS

The spiral arms that fan out from the middle of the building house five themed sections of the aquarium. The unusual spiral design means that there is no fixed route through the building. This means visitors can explore in random and individual ways, which also reduces queues across the aquarium.

The Ocean is the biggest of the five exhibits.

The Lakes of Africa exhibit features dwarf crocodiles.

Amazonas features Europe's largest shoal of piranhas.

The Coral Reef gives visitors a great view of a living coral reef.

The Faroe Islands exhibit includes Nordic sharks, halibut, cod, and catfish.

⟪ Shark tunnel

In the Ocean exhibit, visitors can walk through a 16-m (52-ft) long transparent tunnel with sharks swimming around them. It's the sort of close encounter with ocean predators that is normally only experienced by intrepid divers.

Key features

⩔ The aquarium's biggest tank, the Ocean, contains 4 million litres (1.1 million gallons) of seawater. Visitors can see sharks, rays, groupers, and other creatures through a vast 16 x 8 m (52 x 26 ft) window that is 45 cm (18 in) thick to hold the water back.

A window on the Ocean

⩔ The building's shape was inspired by the swirling water currents of a whirlpool. It also resembles the spiral shape of some seashells. The building is covered with thousands of diamond-shaped aluminium shingles that look like shimmering, silver fish scales.

The Blue Planet from above

The bedrooms and public areas of the hotel are decorated with ice sculptures.

Guests sleeping on the Icehotel's ice-block beds keep warm with reindeer skins and sleeping bags.

ICEHOTEL

One of the coolest places on Earth is the Icehotel in Jukkasjärvi, Sweden, 200 km (124 miles) north of the Arctic Circle. The entire building is made of snow and ice, and lasts over the freezing winter months only. It is redesigned and rebuilt each year using blocks of ice from the nearby River Torne and thousands of tonnes of snow.

HOW IT WORKS

Snow and ice are good heat insulators. People have used snow houses, called igloos, for thousands of years. Inside an igloo, air is warmed by heat rising from a fire or from people's bodies. The thick snow blocks that make the walls of an igloo trap the air, preventing the warmth from escaping too quickly.

Ice-block dome

Stale air leaves through a vent in the top

Dome deflects wind, making it feel less cold inside

Sleeping platform

Warm air rises

Fresh air enters

Fire heats up the air

Building the Icehotel

» Construction begins in November, when ice blocks are placed over a metal structure, and machines are used to blow a slushy mixture of snow and ice, called snice, over them. Snice is denser than snow, provides better insulation, and doesn't melt as quickly.

Frames form the hotel's shape

Basic structure of the Icehotel

« Natural snow is packed over the snice and left to freeze for a couple of days. Compressed by its own weight, the grains of snow and ice form a strong, self-supporting structure. Next, the metal frames are removed and the basic structure of the Icehotel stands on its own.

» More walls are built from blocks of ice that were cut from the river several months earlier and stored in a warehouse at -7°C (20°F). About 3,000 blocks are used, each up to 1 m (3 ft) thick. Water sprayed on the blocks freezes them solid, acting in a similar way to mortar in a brick wall.

Blocks are cut with chainsaws

A peacock sculpture in the Icehotel

« Craftsmen create the hotel's interior. Builders carve blocks of ice into furniture such as beds, tables, and chairs. Artists sculpt to make wonderful likenesses of horses, bears, birds, and other animals. Even the tumblers the guests drink from are made of ice.

Chilly welcome

The Icehotel has about 50 rooms, which are built to different designs each year. Most guests stay for one night. The temperature throughout the hotel is a chilly –5°C to –8°C (18°F–23°F), so thermals are a must.

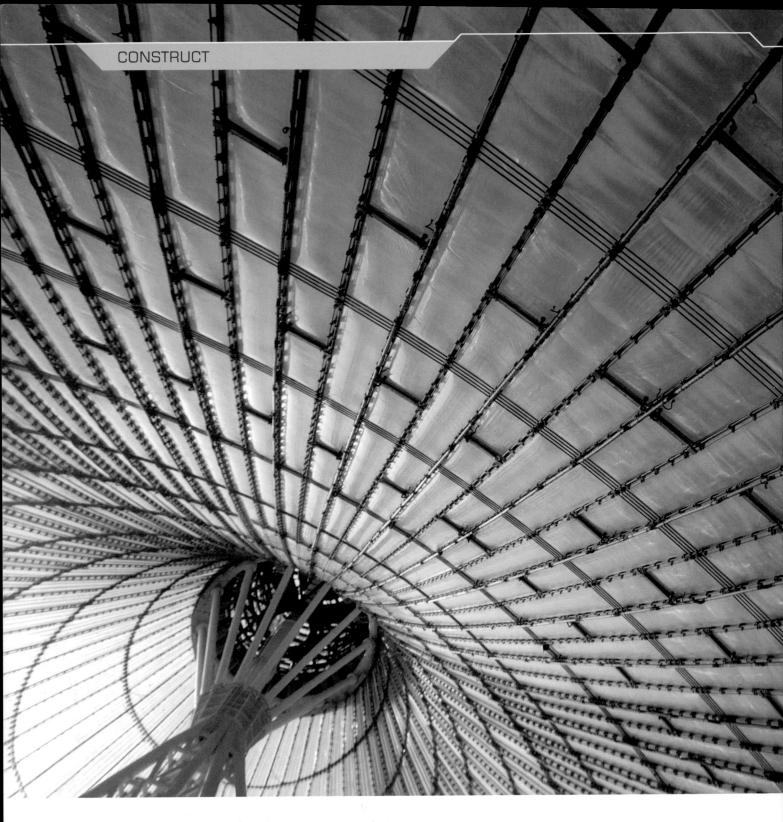

KHAN SHATYR

In 2010, a dramatic new building opened to the public in Nur-Sultan, the capital of Kazakhstan. Its designers had been tasked with creating a giant building with minimum internal support, so they chose a conical tent with a roof made of air-filled plastic cushions. The plastic – ethylene tetrafluoroethylene (ETFE) – is strong, lightweight, and translucent, and hangs from a series of cables that gather at a central spire.

HOW IT WORKS

Nur-Sultan's temperature can plummet to −40°C (−40°F) in winter and soar to more than 35°C (95°F) in summer, so providing a comfortable temperature all year round is quite a challenge. During summer, Khan Shatyr's design makes use of the stack effect, where warm air escapes from the top, which sucks in cold air at the base. In winter, fans blow warm air along the inside of the tent to stop ice forming.

The spire stands on top of a tripod formed from three massive, tubular steel legs.

The roof is anchored to a 20-m (66-ft) high sloping, concrete base.

The roof is supported by a network of steel cables hanging from a tall spire.

Vents in the top of the roof let unwanted hot air escape.

Warm air rising inside the tent draws fresh air in at the bottom.

The interior houses a park, jogging track, shops, and even a tropical beach.

🏠 Tent of the Khan

The Khan Shatyr Entertainment Centre is the world's biggest tent. Its name means "tent of the Khan". The massive structure stands 150 m (492 ft) high and covers an area of more than 100,000 m² (1 million ft²) in the city of Nur-Sultan.

Tower of pillows

The Rocket Tower at the National Space Centre in Leicester, UK, is clad with ETFE – the same material as Khan Shatyr. The 42-m (138-ft) high tower was built to house the centre's biggest exhibits, including its Blue Streak and Thor Able rockets. ETFE was chosen because of its light weight, translucence, and insulation properties. The plastic is in the form of air-filled pillows, each made of three sheets of ETFE welded along their edges. They can be pumped up with more air on colder days to provide better insulation.

National Space Centre Rocket Tower

POMPIDOU CENTRE

Built in the 1970s, the Centre Georges Pompidou, or Pompidou Centre, was not just a new arts centre for Paris, France: it was also a completely new way of designing a building. Its architects, Italian Renzo Piano and Englishman Richard Rogers, wanted to create as much open space inside the building as possible. Their solution was to turn the building inside out and put most of the internal workings of the building – the structural supports, stairways, pipework, lifts, and utilities - that are usually hidden inside, on the outside.

Coloured up

The colourful Pompidou Centre

⌃ The Pompidou Centre makes a feature of its pipes and girders by giving them bright colours that stand out across the city. Colours are used to highlight the functions of the components on the building. The water pipes are green, air pipes are blue, and electrical components are yellow. Red highlights lifts and stairways.

Water pipes in Berlin

⌃ These pink pipes in Berlin, Germany, are a mixture of public works and public art. The city is built on wetland, and large construction sites would flood if the groundwater were not pumped away through this 60-km (37-mile) long network of overhead pipes.

⟫ Glass facade

The front of the Pompidou Centre is a wall of glass, which allows natural light to flood inside by day and creates a vibrant light display at night. Two-thirds of the building's wall surface is covered in a total of 11,000 m² (118,400 ft²) of glass.

Inside out

» The building is supported by a 15,000-tonne box of steel columns and girders. These structural elements are white. The floors are made of reinforced concrete.

» Visitors can enjoy a view over Paris from a glass walkway on the roof. At seven storeys high, the 42-m (138-ft) Pompidou Centre is taller than most of the city's other buildings.

» Most of the Centre's utilities are at the rear of the building. They include water pipes, air pipes, electrical components, lifts, and stairways.

» The front of the building is devoted to transporting visitors. Most travel through the Caterpillar – a set of escalators and walkways inside a tube suspended on the wall.

» Large vents are located on the roof and around the building's base to help keep the 103,305 m² (1,111,966 ft²) floor space inside supplied with fresh air.

BRILLIANT BUILDS

Humans have been building things for thousands of years, but these clever designs show that there are always new things to learn. These amazing projects not only look cool, but their designs often solve problems that more traditional approaches are unable to fix.

Canberra Arboretum

Australia's national tree collection in Canberra is built on 2.5 km² (1 mile²) of land that had been completely destroyed by a bushfire in 2003. In its place, 94 separate forests containing 48,000 trees have been planted on the landscaped hillside. They contain the rarest trees and plants from 100 different countries.

Rolling Bridge

The Rolling Bridge crosses a canal mooring in London, UK. When boats need to pass, it simply rolls up. The bridge's deck is made of eight sections. Pistons inside the bridge's guard wall push hinged sections of the handrails up, which pull the deck into the air. Up and over it goes until the sections form a neat octagon on the far bank.

Microlibrary Bima

With walls made out of 2,000 recycled ice cream tubs, the unique Microlibrary in Bandung, Indonesia, provides local children with books, a dedicated space for reading, and various media facilities for learning activities. It aims to encourage reading, and the ice cream tubs on the walls are arranged to display in binary code a message that reads: "books are the windows to the world".

Telok Blangah

The rugged parklands of Singapore can be enjoyed on foot via a 5-km (3-mile) elevated walkway over steep ravines and through forests. The highlight is the Henderson Waves, a 264-m (866-ft) bridge connecting two hill top parks. The hardwood wave along one side creates shade for walkers, but also drops beneath the deck to offer views of the city.

Rotating house

Sharifi-ha House in Tehran, Iran, changes shape to suit the weather. On cold days, rotating rooms turn so their long sides form the front wall, and inside, the rooms face a covered hallway. In summer, the rooms turn outwards to let the sunshine in. As they turn, the rooms create large spaces for open-air balconies protected by glass barriers.

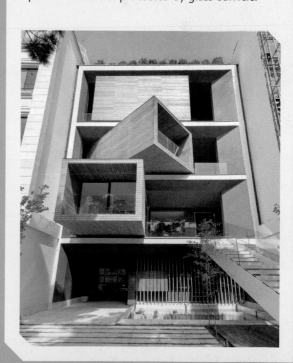

CANTILEVER
BRIDGE

Cantilever bridges are structures that project horizontally over water and are supported on one side only. The advantage of these structures is that they allow crossings over busy waterways. In recent years, designers and engineers have created some particularly innovative cantilever bridges. The 1,000-tonne Scale Lane Bridge, in Hull, UK, is one of them.

HOW IT WORKS

When a large boat is passing, lights flash and bells ring to warn people that the bridge is about to open. The bridge takes a few minutes to retract as it rotates around a 16-m (52-ft) hub, opening up a clear waterway for boats.

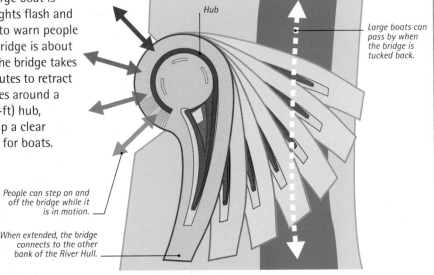

Hub

Large boats can pass by when the bridge is tucked back.

People can step on and off the bridge while it is in motion.

When extended, the bridge connects to the other bank of the River Hull.

Other amazing footbridges

The Loopgraffbrug, The Netherlands

« For centuries, most footbridges were simple arches or beams, but today they are often much more complex and clever structures. The Loopgraafbrug (Trench Bridge), in the Netherlands, floats on the surface of a moat around an 18th-century earth fort. The bridge was designed to be partially submerged because a conventional bridge above the moat would spoil the view of the site.

Capilano Suspension Bridge, Canada

« If you use the Capilano Suspension Bridge near Vancouver, Canada, you should have a good head for heights. Part of the bridge, the Cliff Walk, is suspended 90 m (295 ft) above the ground, on the side of a vertical cliff! Compared to other footbridges, this must be one of the most thrilling walks anywhere in the world.

The moving hub contains a cafe, and sits on a rotating 16-m-(52-ft) diameter ring.

Bridge retracts to allow large boats to pass

Bridge in mid-rotation

Bridge almost connecting to the other side

People can ride on the bridge as it moves along.

≪ Swinging footbridge

The Scale Lane Bridge in Hull, UK, looks like a giant comma reaching out across the river. Its arched underside lets small boats pass underneath. To let larger vessels by, the whole bridge swings out of the way towards one bank.

The 60-m (195-ft) long bridge is a cantilever counterbalanced by a heavy-circular "hub" at one end only.

Design and construction

Floating like a lotus

⌃ A real lotus flower floats on water, so the Lotus Temple is designed to look as if it is floating, too. It is surrounded by nine pools shaped like the floating leaves around the base of a lotus flower. The pools also have a practical purpose – they cool the air that ventilates the building.

Meditation hall

⌃ The Bahá'í faith, which was founded in Persia (modern-day Iran) in the 19th century, endeavours to build beautiful and distinctive places of worship and meditation. The Lotus Temple can accommodate 1,300 worshippers, and the Bahá'í faith allows for the sacred texts of other religions to be read or chanted in their temples.

Interior dome

⌃ It took more than two years to convert the complex curves of the lotus shape into mathematical equations and then structural drawings. To translate the drawings into a physical structure, moulds called formwork were built and filled with concrete. The concrete was then covered with white marble panels from Greece.

The outermost ring of petals forms the nine entrances that encircle the building at ground level.

LOTUS
TEMPLE

On the southwest side of New Delhi, India, a giant white lotus flower towers over the surrounding countryside. This strikingly beautiful structure is actually a temple, a place of worship built by the Bahá'í faith, and is one of India's most-visited attraction with 4.5 million people coming to see it each year.

The petals are made of reinforced concrete that varies in thickness from 6–25 cm (2.4–10 in).

HOW IT WORKS

Delhi can reach temperatures of 45°C (114°F). The Lotus Temple keeps the people inside cool by having openings at the base and the top of the building to draw air up through it naturally.

Pools of water cool air entering the building

Hot air rises and escapes through vents in the roof

Cooler air from outside is drawn in to replace the hot air rising through the vents

⌂ Floral pattern

The Lotus Temple is composed of 27 petal-shaped structures arranged in three concentric circles of nine, forming the shape of a lotus flower. The tips of the innermost petals on top don't meet, forming a glass-covered opening that lets in sunlight.

HOW IT WORKS

The building is designed so that visitors follow a gently sloping ramp that winds around a central open space, or atrium. Radial walls divide the ramp into 70 bays where artwork is displayed. The exterior walls slope outwards at the top, representing the tilt of an artist's easel.

The small rotunda provides extra gallery space.

The large rotunda houses the main exhibition space.

The gently sloping ramp is 400 m (1,312 ft) long.

Restaurant

Small, private film screening room

Open space for social events

Auditorium for talks and performances

Galleries fantastic

The iconic Guggenheim Museum includes a spiralling "drum" shape that houses the primary art gallery. The exterior of this concrete building features dramatic curves and stacked cylinders that set it apart from the surrounding buildings. The museum was renovated in 1992 (when a tower was added), and again from 2005 to 2008.

The Guggenheim, exterior view

Like the Guggenheim, the Tate Modern in London, UK, is a modern art gallery with a surprising design. It is housed in a converted power station beside the River Thames. Its 152-m (500-ft) long Turbine Hall, which once housed the turbines and generators, provides a vast space for giant works of art, and performances.

Turbine Hall, Tate Modern

One of the strangest art galleries is Art on Track. It's the world's largest mobile art gallery. The art is displayed in a passenger train in Chicago, USA. For one day every year, each car of the train is given over to a different artist, or group of artists. The train then circles the Chicago Loop, inviting passengers to hop aboard and enjoy the art.

Art display in Art on Track

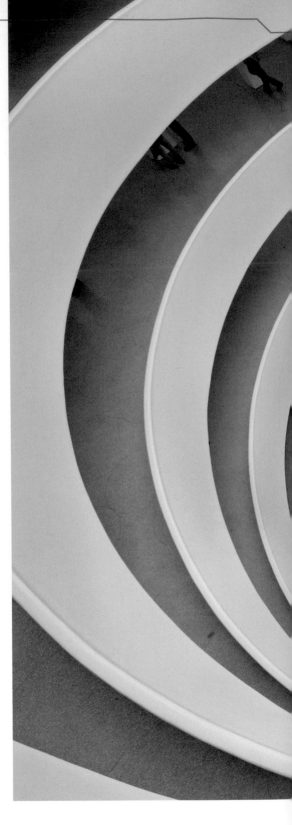

⌃ Distinct design

Despite its unusual design, the large rotunda – wider at the top than the bottom – creates a bright and open space in which to showcase artworks. The spiral path winds around the central atrium, which is where visitors enter the main gallery.

Natural light floods into the atrium from the glass dome above.

Visitors walk along a ramp that spirals up six floors.

ART GALLERY

When the Solomon R. Guggenheim Museum of Modern Art opened in New York City, USA, in 1959, it was unlike any other place in the world. Designed by the famous American architect Frank Lloyd Wright, its unusual shape was controversial, but it quickly became a popular building that influenced other architects.

Hotel floor plan

Hydropolis

Hydropolis will sit in the sea like an artificial island. Part of the giant structure will stand above the surface and the rest will be submerged. A small fleet of water taxis will ferry guests between the hotel and the nearby shore.

Solar panels fixed to the arena's roof generate electricity.

A massive swimming pool will be set inside the hotel.

An arena on the surface hosts shows to entertain guests.

The underwater levels house more than 200 hotel rooms with stunning sea-life views.

FLOATING
HOTEL

Until recently, the idea of people living in the sea was something for science-fiction stories and movies alone. All this may be about to change, however, for there are plans to build the world's first luxury hotel actually in the sea. It's called Hydropolis, meaning "water city", and its vast structure, with more than 200 guest suites, will be anchored to the seabed 20 m (66 ft) below the surface. It will be one of the biggest construction projects of modern times, covering an area of 2.6 km^2 (1 mile^2), and is currently scheduled to be built in Dubai, UAE.

HOW IT WORKS

Hydropolis will work like a vast ship or barge tethered to the seabed by cables. Guests will arrive by ferry at one end of the hotel. From the lobby on the surface they will descend to the three floors that are permanently underwater, giving spectacular views into the surrounding sea. Above the surface, a giant plexiglass roof will give the outdoor areas and walkways some protection from the weather. Part of the roof will be covered with solar panels to generate some of the electricity the hotel will need.

Most of the hotel floors are below the water line.

A plexiglass roof gives shelter and lets light through.

Water taxis dock at jetties.

Cables tether the hotel to the seabed.

Ferries take guests to and from the hotel.

The + Pool

You can do almost anything in New York, USA, except swim in the East River that runs through it because the water is too dirty. The designers of the "+ Pool" (Plus Pool) aim to rectify this by building the world's first water-filtering swimming pool on the river. The floating, cross-shaped, Olympic-sized pool will be equipped with filters to clean 1.9 million litres (500,000 gallons) of river water every day of bacteria and contaminating substances. The water will then flow through the pool, enabling people to swim safely in clean river water.

Plus pool

PALM
JUMEIRAH

The Palm Jumeirah is a set of artificial islands built off the coast of Dubai, United Arab Emirates. It cost $12 billion and took 40,000 workers six years to make. The islands were designed in the shape of a palm branch with 17 fronds, surrounded by a crescent, and constructed from 94 million m³ (3.3 billion ft³) of sand and rock taken from the seabed and desert inland. The Palm Jumeirah is the first of three palm-shaped islands to be constructed, which are set to transform the short desert coastline of Dubai into a city with dozens of beautiful islands and tropical beaches.

Luxurious homes

The seafronts of Palm Jumeirah are devoted to luxury villas and hotel resorts. There is room for 65,000 people to live on the islands. A monorail along the palm's spine brings tourists to their holiday destinations.

Artificial islands

The Palm Jumeirah is the first of several artificial island complexes planned for Dubai. The shapes of the artificial island systems are inspired by nature, and must be carefully planned to ensure that the islands are not washed away during storms.

The Crescent is an 11-km (7-mile) breakwater that shelters the palm islands from rough seas.

The world islands, as seen from space

See the world

All of Dubai's artificial islands are so large that they are visible from space. The latest one is The World, currently under construction along the coast from Palm Jumeirah. Its 300 islands, all for sale as private property, represent the globe's main regions. Once it is completed, the plan is to surround it with yet more islands in a development called The Universe, which will take the shape of the Solar System and the Milky Way.

HOW IT WORKS

Solid is dropped on the seabed to create foundation.

1 The original plan was to use dry desert sand for the foundations, but the sediment dredged from the seabed was found to have better results. The sand foundation is covered in a permeable plastic sheet that holds it in place.

Crescent breakwater foundations

2 The Crescent breakwater is the most robust part of the island construction. The upper layer of its foundations are covered in rocks cut from inland quarries. They create a sloping shoreline that absorbs the energy of waves.

Satellites ensure sand is directed to the correct place.

3 The location of each island was planned precisely to give the system its unique symmetry and to allow water currents to move around the islands. Satellite technology helped pinpoint suitable areas of the seabed to build on.

Sand and seawater mixture blasted into the chosen areas.

4 Large pumps sprayed a mixture of sand and seawater on to the foundations to create the above-water surfaces. This layer was then shaken using vibrating probes to make the sand settle and compact, making it fit to be built on.

Crescent breakwater allows the tides to circulate water through the artificial lagoon.

≫ Mega cutter

Bertha's cutterhead, the disc that covers the entire front end of the machine, is covered in 260 cutting teeth. Their job is to break up rock and earth. The teeth wear away, so they are designed and replaced periodically.

Constructing the tunnel

Tunnel after Bertha has passed through

⌃ The tunnel dug by Bertha is immediately lined with concrete blocks before the weight of the ground above distorts it. Liquid concrete called grout is then pumped behind the blocks to fill any empty spaces. As Bertha bores through the ground, it leaves a stable, waterproof, and perfectly circular tunnel behind.

Upper deck carries southbound traffic

Lower deck carries northbound traffic

Double-decker road tunnel

⌃ When Bertha has completed its work, it will be dismantled and sold, and the tunnel it creates will replace the Alaskan Way Viaduct, which currently handles 110,000 cars every day. Bertha's tunnel will become a two-deck, four-lane road. The empty spaces around the road are used for utility pipes and cables, and emergency pedestrian walkways.

BERTHA

Whenever a new underground road or rail line is needed, a massive tunnel must be dug. To do this, we use a huge tunnel boring machine (TBM). A TBM threads its way through the ground like an enormous mechanical earthworm, grinding up the earth in front of it and spewing the debris behind. It even installs ringed concrete panels, leaving a perfectly circular tunnel behind. The world's largest TBM is a machine known as Bertha. It measures 100 m (328 ft) long and 17.5 m (57 ft) in diameter. It was built in Osaka, Japan, for a 3.2-km (2-mile) tunnelling project in Seattle, USA.

Giant drill

HOW IT WORKS

Bertha is wedged into the tunnel and then the cutterhead is pushed forwards. The cutterhead rotates and its teeth grind the rock away. The broken-up rock falls into a space behind the cutterhead and a conveyor belt carries it away. Next, the jacks wedging Bertha are retracted, and the machine advances into the newly dug space. It wedges itself in place and pushes the cutterhead forwards again.

Cutterhead cuts through rock at a rate of 10 m (35 ft) per day

A shield protects the equipment inside the machine.

The trailing gear contains everything needed to run the machine, which is operated by 25 people.

As it passes through the ground, Bertha installs concrete "rings", which become the tunnel's exterior walls.

A conveyor belt carries debris back to the tunnel's entrance. As the tunnel grows, so does the conveyor belt.

MAGIC MATERIALS

One of the practical benefits of scientific research is its ability to come up with new materials for use in fields such as construction, industry, and medicine. Usually, these new materials are stronger, lighter, or more cost-effective than current materials, but sometimes they have properties that are completely new, leading to new ways of making things.

Super-strong concrete

Concrete is usually reinforced internally by a steel frame. Constructing the frame is time-consuming, so scientists and engineers are testing alternative materials that might be added to concrete to strengthen it. One possibility is adding carbon nanotubes to bind the concrete together. Early tests show the nanotubes help distribute strain well, making the concrete as strong as steel-framed reinforced concrete.

Self-healing concrete

Concrete is one of the most versatile building materials, but it isn't perfect because it can be damaged and crack. The Delft University of Technology in the Netherlands has developed a solution that involves live bacteria. If the concrete cracks, water seeps in and activates the bacteria present in the concrete mix. The water causes the bacteria to produce calcite (limestone), which fills the cracks, and fixes the problem.

Self-cleaning surfaces

Walls and other surfaces attract dirt, germs, and graffiti, and the race is on to make materials that repel dirt. Scientists at the Wyss Institute at Harvard University, USA, have developed a super-efficient self-cleaning material called SLIPS (Slippery Liquid-Infused Porous Surface) that repels almost everything that touches it. This can even stop water from soaking into soft fabrics.

Copying bone

Bones have a honeycomb-like inner framework that makes them strong and light. By copying this structure, researchers at Karlsruhe Institute of Technology in Germany have created a material as strong as steel and lighter than water. It is made by using a laser beam to harden light-sensitive material. A coating of alumina, a tough chemical compound, adds further strength.

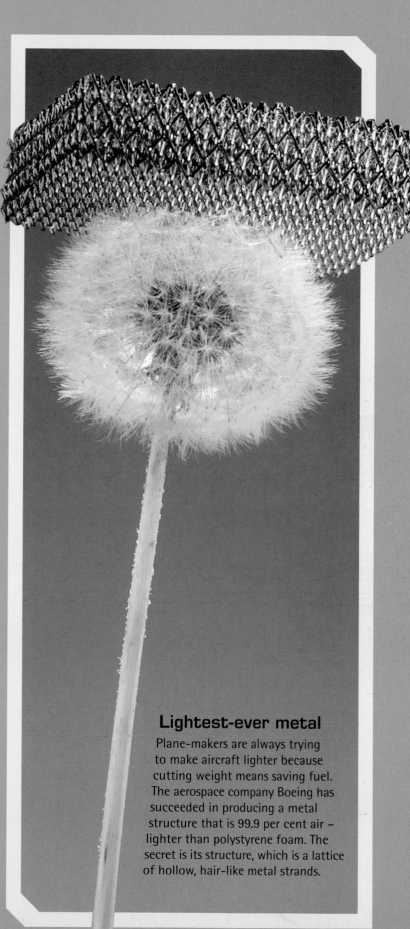

Lightest-ever metal

Plane-makers are always trying to make aircraft lighter because cutting weight means saving fuel. The aerospace company Boeing has succeeded in producing a metal structure that is 99.9 per cent air – lighter than polystyrene foam. The secret is its structure, which is a lattice of hollow, hair-like metal strands.

POWER 4

We need a constant supply of energy every day. The world runs on electricity from power stations to batteries. Traditionally, this electricity was produced by burning fossil fuels, but scientists are developing more environmentally sound ways of making electricity using sunlight and flowing water. Power also means strength, and this chapter covers this, too – whether it's the tiny Raspberry Pi computer, or the massive Bagger 293 bucket-wheel excavator.

HOW IT WORKS

The Gigafactory is powered by energy from the Sun. It is captured by solar panels made of two different layers of impure silicon – called the P-type and N-type layers – sandwiched together. Where the layers meet, a barrier forms, through which electrons can pass in one direction only. When light strikes a panel, some electrons in the silicon become mobile. The barrier then forces them to move through wires connecting the two layers together, creating an electric current.

Glass top layer (cutaway)

1 *Light hits the cell.*

N-type layer

2 *Electrons are knocked loose*

3 *The electrons flow through the circuit, creating electricity.*

At the P-N junction, electrons can only travel from the P-type layer to N-type layer.

4 *Electrons continue their journey to the P-type layer.*

P-type layer

Inside a solar cell

Gigafactory

Tesla's first Gigafactory in Nevada produces as many lithium batteries for cars as all the producers in the rest of the world put together. The factory is powered mostly by its rooftop solar panels.

Other storage units

» It takes several hours to charge a Tesla car battery at home, but it can be charged faster. Tesla's high-speed public superchargers can charge the battery in minutes. A 30-minute supercharge gives the car a range of 275 km (170 miles).

Supercharger

« Tesla's Powerwall is a large battery that stores energy for powering a home. It can be charged by cheap grid electricity or energy from a renewable source such as solar panels. A high-power version called the Powerpack is made for industrial users.

Powerwall

GIGAFACTORY

American car company Tesla plans to produce 500,000 affordable electric cars a year by 2020, but this would require the world's entire current global production of lithium batteries. To supply the batteries they need, Tesla has built a giant factory in Nevada, USA, called the Gigafactory. Manufacturing batteries on this scale has driven production costs down by 30 per cent, making their cars cheaper for consumers.

The total land area is 40 km² (15.5 miles²).

Solar panels and other renewable sources will produce more energy than the factory needs.

HOW IT WORKS

A typical job for Baxter might be picking up parts from a conveyor belt and packing them in a box. Once Baxter is shown how to do the job by a co-worker, it can carry out the task without supervision. Its facial expressions show whether it is struggling or finding the task manageable.

1 *In Baxter's training mode, the trainer can swing the arm to the part that needs to be picked up and the arm button is clicked by the trainer.*

2 *The part is shown on Baxter's screen, and the trainer can confirm that this is the thing to be moved.*

3 *The trainer swings the arm to where the part needs to be placed, and clicks again. One final click tells Baxter that this is the whole task.*

4 *If placed by a conveyor belt, the robot will perform the same task repeatedly, as long as the parts and boxes are in roughly the same place.*

Super senses

» Baxter has a camera in each wrist to give a close-up view of the objects it picks up and handles. The arms can be fitted with a parallel-jaw gripper for general use or a vacuum cup gripper for picking up flat objects.

Gripper with camera

« Baxter's motorized joints are equipped with sensors that detect resistance and collisions. They enable the robot to lessen the force instantly if any of its moving parts bumps into a human, reducing the chance of causing an injury.

Motorized joint

Electric motors move the joints in the arms.

Each of Baxter's arms has a reach of 1.2 m (4 ft).

BAXTER

Baxter is a new kind of robot built to work alongside humans. Instead of being programmed like most robots, Baxter is trained by fellow workers. It can carry out simple tasks such as sorting and loading, without posing any danger to its human co-workers.

A loop of sensors around Baxter's head detects people nearby.

A computer running a special program called Intera 3 controls the robot's movements.

Expressions

Baxter's screen communicates how it "feels" about how the job is going. Baxter can express concentration as it learns a task, and confusion and sadness when it has difficulties.

Neutral

Sleep

Concentration

Focus

Surprise

Confusion

Sadness

Humans can use navigators on the arms and torso to pick options that appear on Baxter's screen.

Industrial robots at work in a factory

Industrial robots

Collaborative robots, or cobots, like Baxter, are different from most industrial robots. Industrial robots are normally used for jobs that are too dangerous, dirty, or dull for humans. They are usually powerful machines used for lifting, welding, or assembling machines like cars.

⌄ Collaborative robot

Baxter is a two-armed robot designed to help with simple jobs such as loading, handling, and sorting materials. It stands almost 2 m (6.5 ft) tall. Baxter is operated by a standard personal computer mounted in its chest.

A gripper at the end of the arm can pick things up and move them around.

RASPBERRY PI

The Raspberry Pi is as simple as a personal computer gets. Designed as a small motherboard (a circuit board that has all the basic elements of a computer), the Raspberry Pi is a fraction of the price of even a basic desktop computer. The Pi has no internal hard disk, and all software is stored on a Secure Digital (SD) card created especially to control the computer. It can play videos, connect to the Internet, and run everyday applications. Also, its low cost and small size makes the Raspberry Pi ideal as a programming tool, used to create your own games and music, control home-made robots, or whatever else you can dream up.

HOW IT WORKS

As well as working like a regular computer, the Raspberry Pi is built to connect to all kinds of other devices. These are known as HATs, short for "Hardware Attached on Top" because they are sized to screw in place over the motherboard. A HAT can carry any device, from altitude detectors to thermometers. This robot car is controlled by a program running on the Raspberry Pi inside while connected to a HAT. The HAT drives the motors on each wheel and is connected to detectors that tell the robot what is around it.

Chip containing quad-core processor

Display connector for linking to LCD screens, such as televisions

Software loaded via a micro-SD card slot on underside

USB-C port used for power supply

Micro-HDMI ports connect to 4K (Ultra HD) TV or monitor

Raspberry Pi and HAT wired into robot car

Each wheel is spun by an electric motor controlled by the HAT.

Ultrasonic sensors detect objects around the car.

HAT board

Wi-Fi antenna connects Raspberry Pi to control computer

A computer that fits on your palm

Tiny yet functional

Despite being not much bigger than a bank card, the Raspberry Pi is a fully functioning computer. It can be connected to an everyday television screen and works with any mouse and keyboard.

Input-output pins send and receive commands to and from other devices

Camera Serial Interface (CSI) connects to camera by a flat ribbon cable

Hackaball

The Hackaball is a computer that has been designed as a fun way of introducing children to the basics of computer programming. By using an app, kids can design and program their own games for the ball – such as "pass the bomb" or "keepie-uppie" – by setting up a simple set of rules and instructions. It is tough enough to be bounced, thrown, kicked, and rolled, and is also sensitive to motion and can change colour, vibrate, and make sounds. The Hackaball can be reprogrammed – meaning the instructions can be changed – to improve and alter the games available.

Hackaball is part toy, part programming device

RAM chip containing 1 GB, 2 GB, or 4 GB of memory

Gigabit Ethernet socket connects to a wired computer network

Two USB 3.0 ports allow high-speed data transfer

Two USB 2.0 ports can connect to peripheral equipment, such as a mouse, keyboard, or Wi-Fi antenna

3.5 mm (0.1 in) jack for audio and video connections

HOW IT WORKS

The excavator's bucket wheel is attached to a boom that is connected to a central platform. The position of the bucket wheel can be changed by the boom. When operated, the bucket wheel is lowered into the ground, and it slowly cuts into the earth. As the buckets rotate, the earth is deposited on to a conveyor belt that carries it along the boom and away for processing.

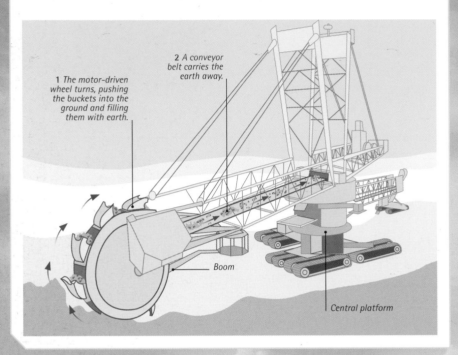

1 The motor-driven wheel turns, pushing the buckets into the ground and filling them with earth.

2 A conveyor belt carries the earth away.

Boom

Central platform

The wheel has giant buckets around its edge that tear into the ground and scoop earth up.

Other big diggers

Bucket-wheel excavators are not suitable for every digging job. There are other giant diggers for these jobs. The biggest single-bucket diggers are draglines. These machines lower a huge bucket to the ground and drag it back towards the digger, scooping up earth on the way. Smaller excavators move on tracks or wheels, but big machines like the Caterpillar 8750 walk on giant feet!

Caterpillar 8750

🔺 Mammoth digger

This giant bucket-wheel excavator is used at a mine in Germany. Each of its buckets is as big as a family car. The biggest of these machines can dig up to 240,000 m³ (8.5 million ft³) of coal a day, or enough to fill 96 Olympic swimming pools.

A wide base spreads the immense weight of the machine over a large area to stop it from sinking.

BUCKET-WHEEL
EXCAVATOR

In places where coal lies close to the surface, the most efficient way to reach it is to strip away the soil and rock that lies on top of it. Machines called bucket-wheel excavators are often used for this task, and they are some of the biggest land vehicles ever built. The largest of these is the Bagger 293. From end to end it measures 225 m (738 ft) and stands 96 m (315 ft) tall. It tips the scales at a whopping 14,200 tonnes, making it the world's heaviest land vehicle.

The battery pack has a life of up to six hours.

Four motors move the hips and each knee.

The exoskeleton can be strapped on in less than five minutes.

A computer analyses data from 15 sensors to control the legs.

BIONIC SUIT

Injuries to the spinal cord can be catastrophic. Depending on the location and severity of the injury, it can mean a lifetime as a wheelchair user. Other conditions, such as a stroke, can cause weakness in the legs that makes walking difficult. American company Ekso Bionics' powered exoskeletal (external skeleton) suit is designed to help people with these problems. Originally conceived as a device to give people superhuman strength for lifting heavy loads, powered exoskeletons can also enable wheelchair-bound people to walk again.

Exoskeletons in nature

Nature invented the exoskeleton, long before engineers thought of it. Animals such as crabs, lobsters, beetles, and spiders all have exoskeletons. The hard exterior protects the creature from predators, but it makes growth difficult. To grow, the animal must shed its exoskeleton to develop a new, bigger one.

Ironclad beetle

The leg length can be adjusted to suit the wearer's body shape.

≫ Walking unassisted

The Ekso exoskeleton is a wearable robot. It straps to the waist, shoulders, and legs, together with a backpack containing the suit's computerized control system and batteries. The exoskeleton can be operated by a therapist using a remote control until the wearer gets the hang of using it. After building muscle power, the user can take control and walk unassisted.

The path of each foot is adjusted 500 times a second to prevent stumbling.

Extra support

The Ekso suit can be used with a variety of additional supportive equipment to help get its wearer upright and walking. A walking frame, crutches, or a walking stick can give the extra support needed until the wearer is able to walk unaided.

A rundown of the main experiments

CMS

⌃ The Compact Muon Solenoid (CMS) is one of two general-purpose particle detectors in the LHC, the other being ATLAS. CMS was used in the successful search for the Higgs boson particle, and is crucial in dark matter studies and the search for possible extra dimensions.

LHC-b

⌃ LHC-b is used to investigate why there seems to be much more matter than anti-matter in the Universe. Equal amounts should have been produced by the Big Bang, but matter dominates the Universe today. The "b" in LHC-b stands for "beauty".

ATLAS

⌃ ATLAS stands for A Toroidal LHC ApparatuS. It has the same goals as the CMS detector, but it uses different equipment and methods. It tracks the path, momentum, and energy of particles that fly out of proton collisions.

ALICE

⌃ A Large Ion Collider Experiment (ALICE) was built to study how tiny particles called quarks combined to form the larger subatomic particles like protons and neutrons that we see today. To find this out, ALICE mashes lead nuclei, and not protons, together.

HOW IT WORKS

A series of accelerators boost the speed of subatomic protons until they can be injected into the LHC. Two beams of protons in side-by-side tubes circle in opposite directions. The beams cross at four places – CMS, LHC-b, ATLAS, and ALICE – where different experiments record the results of collisions between the particles.

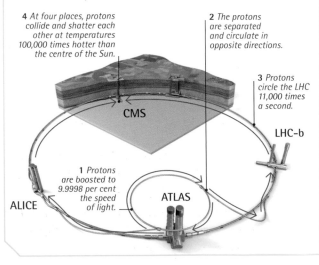

4 At four places, protons collide and shatter each other at temperatures 100,000 times hotter than the centre of the Sun.

2 The protons are separated and circulate in opposite directions.

3 Protons circle the LHC 11,000 times a second.

1 Protons are boosted to 9.9998 per cent the speed of light.

CMS

LHC-b

ALICE

ATLAS

LARGE HADRON
COLLIDER

The Large Hadron Collider (LHC) is the largest and most complex scientific instrument ever built. It studies the science of subatomic particles by speeding them up to almost the speed of light before smashing them together, to see the even smaller bits that are flung out. The energy released in these collisions are like miniature recreations of the Big Bang.

⌃ An underground giant

Looking like the inside of a high-tech washing machine, this is the Compact Muon Solenoid (CMS), a detector in the Large Hadron Collider. It is 15 m (49 ft) wide, weighs 14,000 tonnes, and is housed in a cavern 100 m (328 ft) below ground.

LIGHTEN UP

Light is a very useful, and free, source of energy, and inventors are busy creating new products that use it and produce it. They use solar panels to change light into electricity, and they concentrate light with mirrors so that it generates high temperatures. They've also discovered how to make a brand new material called graphene produce light.

Solar pavilion

To show off the V60, their hybrid electric/petrol car, Swedish car company Volvo designed a collapsible pavilion that featured solar panels. The beautiful pavilion can fold up to fit in the boot, meaning it can be used to charge the car wherever you go.

GoSun

The GoSun solar stove uses nothing more than sunlight to produce temperatures high enough to cook food. Food is placed on a long, thin tray, which slides inside a glass tube. Reflectors focus sunlight on the tube and heat it up. The stove can cook a meal in 20 minutes at a temperature of up to 288°C (550°F).

Revolights

Being seen by other road users is important for cyclists. Revolights make bikes easy to see by lighting up light emitting diodes (LEDs) on the wheels, white at the front and red at the back. The system detects the bike's speed and lights the LEDs only when they are at the front of the front wheel and the back of the rear wheel.

Solar-powered socket

There are lots of solar-powered batteries and chargers, but this product is the first solar-powered socket. When it is stuck to a sunlit window, a solar panel on the sticky side generates electricity and charges a built-in 1,000 mAh battery. A phone, tablet, or other device can be plugged into a socket on the other side of the unit.

Graphene bulb

Researchers have discovered how to make a light bulb from the new wonder material, graphene, an ultra-thin honeycombed form of carbon. When an electric current flows through a strip of graphene, heat is generated. It can reach a temperature of up to 2,530°C (4,590°F) and glow brightly. In the future, this could help microchips communicate with each other by using light.

SOFTROCKER

Relaxing in a shady sunlounger on a summer's day can recharge your batteries in more ways than one. Architects at the Massachusetts Institute of Technology (MIT) in the United States have come up with a way of using the Sun to charge your gadgets while you crash out in comfort. Knowing that sunshades soak up solar energy, which then goes to waste, MIT students helped to design a lounger that would make use of this free energy. The result is the SOFT Rocker, a futuristic piece of outdoor furniture that generates free electricity while you lounge.

Solar windows

Electricity-generating plastic

Most of the solar energy that reaches Earth's surface is wasted. If more solar panels were used in construction, buildings could generate electricity in the same way as the SOFT Rocker. Researchers working on ways of harnessing sunlight have developed an electricity-generating plastic panel. Just one skyscraper clad in this new material would make a vast amount of electricity.

The solar panels generate electricity to charge a battery.

Tracking the Sun

The SOFT Rocker gently rocks and rotates as the person inside it shifts position. By adjusting the rocker's angle, the sitter can lounge comfortably in the shade while keeping the solar panels directly facing the Sun.

Using free energy

Charging a smartphone

⌃ State-of-the-art thin-film solar panels on top of the SOFT Rocker charge a 6-volt, 12 amp-hour battery. This battery can charge up to three phones at the same time in about four hours and can top up many other electronic devices, too. It also stores energy taken in during the day, so it can be used at any time, even at night. The SOFT Rocker's curvy shape is designed to hold the solar panels at the right angle for maximum Sun exposure on the MIT campus, but could be adapted for any site.

The SOFT Rocker as night falls

⌃ After dark, the SOFT Rocker's battery powers an electroluminescent (EL) strip inside the lounger. The strip is made of a semiconducting material that can be cut to any length. It lights up when an electric current from the Rocker's battery flows through it. Like a light emitting diode (LED), the strip produces light without heat, bathing the lounger in a soft coloured glow.

JET ENGINE

With more than 50,000 in action across the globe, the Rolls-Royce company is world-famous for its jet engines. The Trent is one of its most successful engine families, powering the Airbus and Boeing aeroplanes. The latest model is the Trent 7000, developed for the new Airbus A330 neo twin-engine airliner. It is about 50 per cent quieter and 10 per cent more fuel-efficient than previous Trent engines.

HOW IT WORKS

The spinning fan sucks in enough air to fill a squash court every second. A compressor squeezes it to one-fiftieth of its volume. Burning fuel heats it to 1,600°C (2,900°F). The gas expands rapidly, jetting out of the engine through the turbine, helping to propel the aeroplane forward.

1 The 2.8-m (9.1-ft), 20-bladed fan spins, sucking air into the engine.

3 Ninety per cent of the air from the fan passes straight through the engine.

5 The hot gas leaves the engine through the turbine and generates thrust, helping to force the aeroplane forward.

4 Fuel burns in the combustion chamber to create hot gas, which expands rapidly.

2 Ten per cent of the fan air is squashed by a compressor.

Marine turbines

Queen Elizabeth Class aircraft carrier

Trent engines are not only found on airliners. A variant of the Trent, the Marine Trent, powers warships. Instead of producing a jet of gas to thrust an aircraft through the sky, the Marine Trent uses its power to turn a ship's propellers to move the ship forward. The British Royal Navy's newest aircraft carriers, the Queen Elizabeth Class, are powered by the Marine Trent. These ships, at a weight of 65,000 tonnes, are the biggest surface ships ever operated by the Royal Navy.

⌂ Air power

The big, 20-bladed fan at the front of the Trent 7000 gives this type of engine its name – turbofan. The spinning fan generates three-quarters of the engine's thrust. Only 10 per cent of the air from the fan enters the engine's hot core.

HYDROELECTRIC
DAM

Hydroelectric dams are massive concrete structures that generate electricity by using energy extracted from moving water. The biggest in the world is the Three Gorges Dam in Hubei, China. Standing across the mighty Yangtze River, its 34 turbines can generate 20 times the energy output of a nuclear power station. There were proposals for a dam on the Yangtze to generate electricity and control flooding as long ago as 1919, but onstruction didn't actually begin until 1994. It was completed 14 years later, in 2008, and became fully operational in 2012.

Trash collection

Though the dam is seen as a modern wonder, an unavoidable downside is that it collects everything thrown into the river. Three tonnes of rubbish is removed every day. During the rainy season, it can get so bad that people can walk across the rubbish islands that develop.

Collecting rubbish in the reservoir

HOW IT WORKS

1 Water from the reservoir enters a huge pipe called a penstock. This guides the water downhill, gathering speed, towards the power plant's turbines.

2 The fast-flowing water hits the blades of a row of turbines. The water transfers some of its energy to the turbines, making them spin at high speed.

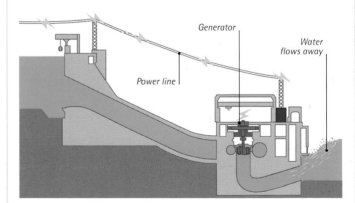

3 Each turbine is connected to a generator. The spinning turbine drives the generator. This produces electricity, which is carried away by power lines.

❮ Water power in action

China's Three Gorges Dam is 2.3 km (1.4 miles) long and 181 m (594 ft) high. Water from the reservoir behind the dam drives its turbines, producing 22,500 megawatts of electricity. A lift allows large ships to traverse the dam.

5 LIVE

There are countless appliances of all kinds that help make our lives easier, longer, or more enjoyable. Thanks to some clever thinking, it is now possible for each of us to carry thousands of books with us at all times, see through bionic eyes, and even teach our pets to play electronic games. Scientists and engineers are not just looking at ways of making life on Earth better, though. They are working on the technology that will allow us one day to leave the planet to also live on our neighbour, Mars.

C-THRU HELMET

Though their name suggests they only battle flames, firefighters have another, more dangerous, foe, in the form of smoke. When dense smoke fills enclosed spaces, visibility is zero, and firefighters have to find their way around by touch and hearing. Nobody inside a burning building can survive beyond a few minutes in the choking atmosphere, including those trying to rescue people. Using a combination of brilliant technologies, a concept helmet called the C-Thru has been designed to give firefighters some crucial advantages over current equipment when out trying to save people's lives.

Optical thermal camera

3-D data on visor

Exhalation vent

Wireless data transmitter

Air hose

The wearer is able to stay in touch with other firefighters through the helmet.

Hi-tech helmet

Easy to wear

Firefighters usually need to be ready for action in 90 seconds after a call, so the C-Thru Helmet is designed to be put on quickly and easily, even at night in a fire engine going at full speed.

Seeing through the smoke

The C-Thru Smoke Diving Helmet aims to provide firefighters with all of the information they need to find people in burning buildings, without the need to carry extra equipment. Firefighters who primarily work inside burning buildings are called "smoke divers".

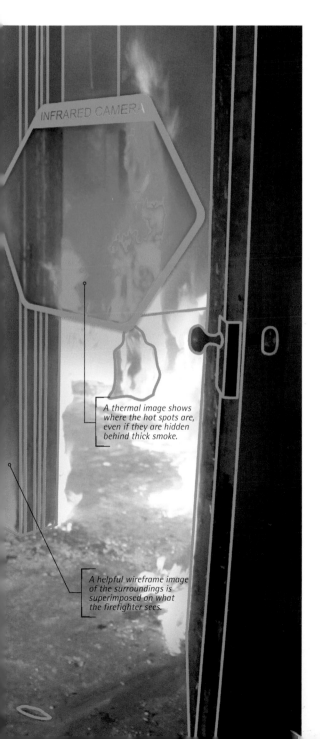

INFRARED CAMERA

A thermal image shows where the hot spots are, even if they are hidden behind thick smoke.

A helpful wireframe image of the surroundings is superimposed on what the firefighter sees.

HOW IT WORKS

The C-Thru Helmet includes image processing, communication, and audio systems. An optical thermal camera on the front of the helmet captures image data from the situation. The data is transmitted to a device held by the firefighters' team leader outside the building. This device processes the data and transmits it back to the firefighters' helmets, which project it on the visor. To improve hearing as well as vision, the helmet's audio system cancels the sound of the wearer's breathing and unimportant noise.

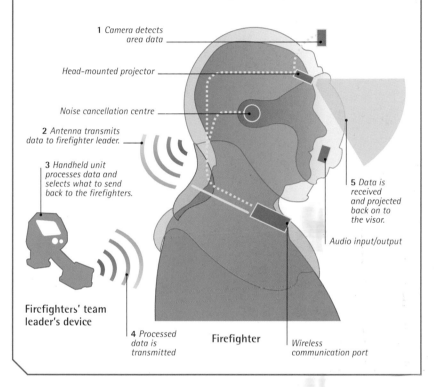

1 *Camera detects area data*

Head-mounted projector

Noise cancellation centre

2 *Antenna transmits data to firefighter leader.*

3 *Handheld unit processes data and selects what to send back to the firefighters.*

5 *Data is received and projected back on to the visor.*

Audio input/output

Firefighters' team leader's device

4 *Processed data is transmitted*

Firefighter

Wireless communication port

Armoured divers

Like firefighters, people who venture into other extreme environments have to wear protective clothing and life support systems. One of the most dangerous places on Earth is at the bottom of an ocean. The pressure of the water will crush divers to death unless they are protected by an atmospheric diving suit. Resembling a suit of armour, this enables a diver to breathe and work at depths of 600 m (2,000 ft). At this level, pressure is 60 atmospheres: 60 times the atmospheric pressure at the surface of the sea.

A diver in an atmospheric diving suit

CLEVERPET

Just like people, animals get bored when they have nothing to do. The answer for owners who have to leave their dogs alone at home could be an electronic device called CleverPet. This is a games console that uses lights and sound to give dogs various puzzles to solve, with tasty rewards for correct responses. Puzzles include remembering sequences of lights and responding to audio cues.

Touchscreen-like interactive pads light up.

HOW IT WORKS

For the light-sequence game, the machine plays a pattern of flashing lights. The dog must then touch the pads in the right order, which is registered by the pads. If the dog gets a sequence right, a mechanism called a worm gear, consisting of a threaded screw and a toothed wheel, drives round a food tray carrying a titbit. The dog takes the reward and the tray rotates out of sight again. Inside the dome, another treat drops on to the tray, ready for the next game.

1 *Touch pad lights up.*

2 *Dog responds*

3 *Tray appears with food treat if the dog presses the correct pad.*

4 *CleverPet's software changes the game to keep the dog interested.*

⋙ Work for idle paws

CleverPet's games include encouraging the dog to remember a sequence of lights, respond to audio commands, or touch the lights when they flash. As the dog learns, the games get faster and more difficult, with new games available to download via Wi-Fi.

The food tray is hidden until the dog presses the correct touchpad. Then it rotates into view with a treat for the dog to eat.

The dome contains a food hopper that holds two or three cups of dry dog food.

Smart gadgets for pets

⋙ Pet owners can choose from a variety of smart gadgets designed especially for animals. One of these devices, called WÜF, is a sort of activity tracker for dogs. Worn like a collar, it tracks the dog using GPS and also monitors the dog's daily activities. Using an app and a smartphone, an owner can talk to a dog via a loudspeaker in the collar, and the dog's bark back can be heard because WÜF also has a built-in microphone.

The collar comes in different sizes to suit the dog.

WÜF collar

A GPS antenna tracks location.

⋙ It's not just dogs that are having all of the techie fun. Cats can get in on the act with the FroliCat Bolt, a laser toy that shines a bright moving dot on the floor for the cat to chase and pounce on. The random laser patterns are designed to stimulate a cat's natural hunting instincts. An automatic timer switches the toy off after 15 minutes of feline fun. These sorts of playthings are designed to give cats exercise and entertainment, especially if they live indoors all the time.

A mirror aims the laser beam at a nearby surface.

The laser beam moves around.

FroliCat Bolt

ROTATING HOUSE

The D*Dynamic house is probably the strangest and coolest home you'll ever see. It can change shape to suit the weather! It is a rotating home designed for places that experience extreme temperatures – hot summers and freezing winters. During the cold winter months, it can be arranged as a square, with thick external walls and small windows to conserve heat. In summer, it opens up like a flower and turns inside out, with its glass panels facing outwards to let in plenty of light.

Dynamic buildings

Buildings that move are likely to become a more common part of city skylines in the future. A few have been built already. A building called Suite Vollard in Curitiba, Brazil, is the world's first rotating apartment block. Its circular floors rotate around a static core. Each floor takes an hour to go round once. The windows are tinted blue, gold, and silver, so the building is very eye-catching as the floors rotate in different directions.

Suite Vollard, Brazil

Big windows give panoramic views in warm weather.

Solar panels use sunlight on the roof to generate electricity for the house.

The house of tomorrow

The amazing, shape-shifting D*Dynamic house rotates on special rails set into the ground. It doesn't take much effort to rearrange the layout of the house to suit the occasion.

HOW IT WORKS

The house is divided into four parts shaped according to a formula worked out by the English mathematician Henry Ernest Dudeney. In 1908, he discovered that these four shapes can be arranged to make a perfect square and then rearranged to make a triangle. The parts of the house are linked together and stand on rails so that they can rotate around each other. As the building moves, doors transform into windows and internal walls become external walls. There are eight possible configurations of the house.

The parts rotate around pivot points.

Winter structure

The largest piece rotates out from the centre.

Spring structure

When another section is rotated out, the house is opened up.

Summer structure

The house is now a triangle.

Autumn structure

Rails on circular tracks form a perfectly level base for the various parts of the house to move on.

LOON

Access to the Internet is a luxury in remote parts of the world. This is where Loon comes in. Loon is a network of helium balloons that can take wireless data signals from a mobile operator in one place, and transmit them to users on the ground at another. It enables users to get a high-speed connection to the Internet, even in the world's most isolated areas. The balloons can hover as high as 20 km (12.4 miles) above Earth's surface, and are designed to fly for up to 100 days.

The balloon is made of polyethylene sheets.

« Strong and sturdy

Each Loon is about the size of a tennis court. The balloons are made of a special type of plastic that makes them light and durable. They can withstand temperatures as low as -90°C (-194°F) and winds as fast as 100 kph (62 mph).

Launching Loon

The autolauncher fills a Loon balloon with helium gas

The Loon team designed a launcher that can inflate and launch a balloon into Earth's atmosphere roughly every 30 minutes. The "autolauncher" is a tall crane-like structure, measuring almost 17 m (55 ft) in height. Its side panels protect the balloons from the wind by enclosing them from three sides while being inflated. The launcher releases the balloons smoothly by changing its position to match the direction of the wind.

HOW IT WORKS

The balloons go up into the stratosphere, the layer in Earth's atmosphere that extends from 20–50 km (12–31 miles) above the planet's surface. Each balloon's direction and height are controlled by a computer system on the ground. The balloons can be moved together to cover areas where Internet access is needed. A mobile network tower on the ground sends wireless signals up to the Loon system. One balloon receives the signals, then passes them on across the network. The signals are finally beamed to the ground where mobile devices can connect to the Internet.

Stratosphere

Loon system

20 km
(12.4 miles)

2. Antennas on the balloon transmit the signals to other balloons in the network.

3. Internet signals are transmitted to the ground.

9.6 km
(6 miles)

Aeroplane
9 km (5.7 miles)

Mt Everest
8.8 km (5.5 miles)

1. An internet operator sends signals to the nearest balloon.

⟫ Electronic paper close-up

This false-colour scanning electron microscope (SEM) image shows a rupture in electronic paper, the screen technology used in e-readers. The green lumps are charged e-ink particles, which are arranged into recognizable patterns of text or simple pictures using an electric field.

E-READER

Using an e-reader is an alternative way to read a book. It is small and light enough to hold like a book, but unlike a book, it will never run out of text. When you finish one story, you can simply load or download another. The e-reader's screen displays words in the text from books using e-ink, which works in the same way as physical ink: we can see it because it reflects light from its surroundings. This is different to the screens of a tablet computer or smartphone, which produce their own light and can be tiring to look at for long periods.

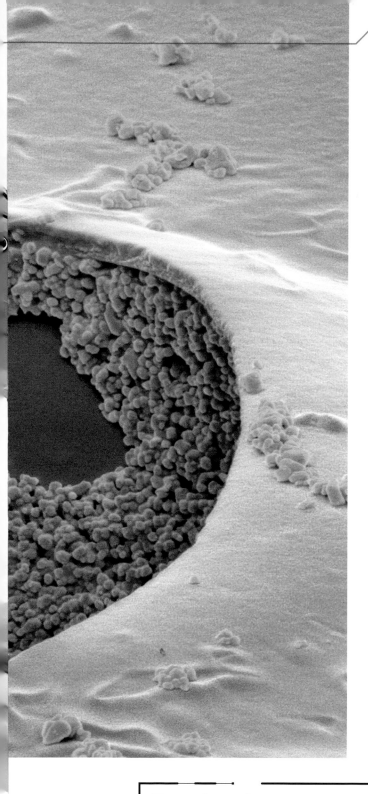

HOW IT WORKS

E-ink devices display text using patterns of black and white dots made by particles inside oil-filled microcapsules. Each microcapsule is the width of a hair, and there are nearly 800,000 of them sandwiched between the transparent screen surface and an electrode. The e-reader sends an instruction in the form of an electric charge to every microcapsule each time the page is changed, causing the ink to show or disappear.

Transparent screen

Negatively charged black particles rise to top of capsule

Positive white particles are attracted to the electrode.

1 A negative charge on electrode makes a black dot appear on screen.

2 Changing the electric charge makes the particles rearrange inside the capsule.

Dots of white particles make the screen brighter and the black text patterns stand out better.

Top of capsule is half white and half black, which is seen as grey.

Negatively charged black particles are pulled down to the electrode.

3 A positive charge on the electrode makes a white dot on screen.

4 A split charge on the capsule creates a grey dot.

E-reader advantages

As well being able to download and store many books, e-readers have other advantages over paper. Many e-readers can be controlled by touch, with the ability to make notes and send text to friends a standard feature. The size of the e-ink text can be adjusted to suit a reader's eyesight, and the typeface can also be changed. The latest e-readers also have small LEDs located at the edge of the screen that are pointed towards the screen. These light the text from the front (not the back like a computer screen), enabling the device to be read in the dark.

Touchscreen e-reader

Pacey's Luck

Not many people know the story of Charlie Pacey – perhaps the most unique person I've ever had the honour of meeting. Every morning he got up, had a full breakfast, and left the house before the sparrows were up.

kindle

ACTIVITY
TRACKER

An activity tracker is a fitness aid that can help you maintain healthy exercise levels. Mostly worn on the wrist, or clipped to clothing, the tracker detects a person's motion. That data is combined with personal information, such as age, height, and weight, by the tracker's software to create a picture of a person's overall health and exercise levels. Activity trackers calculate how many calories you have burned each day, which is useful information for people wanting to lose weight and keep fit. Some trackers worn against the skin can also measure heart rate, by detecting tiny colour changes in the skin as the blood surges through it.

Cooling bracelet

This Wristify device helps keep the body at a comfortable temperature. The gadget is still in development, but it is being designed to make use of a simple trick to cool, or warm, the body. It directs cool air on to the wrist, which chills the skin there. This makes the whole body seem to cool down so the wearer feels more comfortable. The bracelet will glow blue when cooling, or orange when providing a warming effect.

Wristify bracelet

HOW IT WORKS

⌃ Trackers can record sleep length and quality by recording movement as you sleep. This information can help you to get more from your rest.

⌃ Trackers sync their data to smartphone apps, usually via Bluetooth. The apps make it possible to analyse the data to see how you're doing.

⌃ The easiest way to measure activity is by counting a person's footsteps. Motion sensors in the trackers can work out the rhythm and speed of your steps.

⌃ Optical sensors in some trackers can detect the rate of blood flow through the skin. Heart rate data is used to show how hard you are working during exercise.

⌃ Some trackers allow you to show your intended route on their screen, and use the Global Positioning System (GPS) to show where you are on a map.

Garmin vivofit2

This Garmin vivofit2 activity tracker is programmed to set daily activity goals for its wearer, based on his or her past fitness level. A red bar appears on the display when the wearer has been sitting down for an hour or more. Taking a short walk will clear that alert.

The display shows the number of steps made that day.

⌃ Fitness Band

Activity trackers are crammed with sensors that measure all sorts of things – such as your speed, heart rate, physical position, and altitude. The real magic happens with the software that takes this information to build a profile of your activity.

PANONO

The Panono is a digital camera that takes pin-sharp images of everything in every direction to create a spherical 360-degree panorama. The 480-g (17-oz) camera can be held in the hand or on a selfie stick, but for best results it should be thrown into the air. An onboard accelerometer tracks the camera's trajectory and takes the photos at the highest point. The images are then viewed through an app, which displays the scene in every direction.

Edible camera

When a doctor needs to look at someone's digestive system, he or she can use a new type of camera. The device is the size of a large pill, and therefore small enough to swallow. Once inside, the camera lights up your insides using powerful LEDs, and records what it sees on video – all the way through to the other end. Once out, the video is available for download, giving the doctor useful clues as to what's wrong.

Swallowable camera

HOW IT WORKS

The ball is encased in a tough plastic shell to protect it if dropped.

The force of the throw determines when the picture is taken.

Throw force pushes the ball upwards

Cameras point in all directions.

Gravity pulls the ball back to Earth

Each camera takes an image that slightly overlaps with those of other cameras.

The ball slows down as it approaches its highest point.

The device can store 600 panoramic shots.

Moving the tablet around reveals the scene in every direction.

1 The throw mode on the ball's control button is selected, and then the camera is tossed upwards. As the Panono launches, its accelerometer measures its initial speed and direction.

2 The force of gravity that slows the ball's trajectory is a constant, and the onboard processor uses that to calculate how high the ball will travel, given its launch speed.

3 At the highest point of the throw, the camera becomes motionless in the air for an instant. This allows the 36 cameras to capture images with the minimum of blur.

4 To view the images, they must be downloaded via a cable or through Wi-Fi, and the app combines them into a 360-degree spherical panorama that really captures the whole scene.

❮❮ Capturing the scene

The Panono photographs things around it using 36 cameras. To get the best view, the device is thrown straight up. Each camera takes a shot in the same instant, and they are stitched together into a single image that can be viewed via an app.

LIVING ON
MARS

People could be living on Mars, the "Red Planet", by the 2030s. A typical Mars mission will take about three years, longer than any human has been away from Earth before. After a flight lasting six to eight months, astronauts will spend about 500 days on Martian soil before their journey home. Their base camp buildings, the spacesuits they will wear, and the vehicles they will use for exploration are all currently being developed and tested.

A base built from Martian soil could protect pioneer settlers from deadly radiation.

⩔ The first humans on Mars will arrive on a NASA Orion spacecraft. Orion, designed for travelling in deep space, is currently being tested.

Getting there

⩔ Astronauts on Mars will grow fresh vegetables in a "space garden" like this. They will take fertilizer from Earth to add to the nutrient-poor Martian soil.

Growing greens

Staying healthy

Travelling to Mars and living on the planet could pose serious health risks for astronauts. One major problem is the low gravity on Mars. Without normal Earth gravity to work against, the human body loses muscle tone and bones become weaker. The best remedy is vigorous daily exercise, as astronauts on the International Space Station know all too well. They spend up to two hours a day working out on various exercise machines – running, cycling, and lifting weights.

An ISS astronaut works out

Building a Martian base

Conditions on Mars are lethal to humans, so manned Martian outposts will be safe shelters on a dangerous world. The atmosphere is unbreathable and extremely cold, and the planet is bombarded with deadly radiation from space.

ASTRONAUTS ON MARS – A TIMETABLE

The NASA-planned journey to Mars has three phases. The Earth Reliant Phase, lasting up to the 2020s, is already under way. This stage involves research by the International Space Station into equipment and the effects of long spaceflights on the human body. During the Proving Ground Phase (2020s), missions will go as far as the Moon to test the Mars spacecraft and other technology. Finally, the Earth Independent Phase (2030s) will use the Moon's surface as a base for trials of the buildings and techniques that will be used for life on Mars.

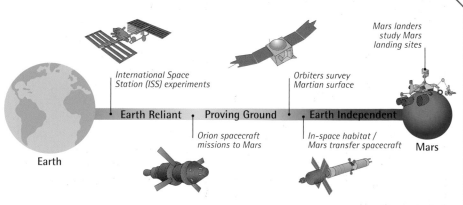

International Space Station (ISS) experiments

Orbiters survey Martian surface

Mars landers study Mars landing sites

Earth Reliant   Proving Ground   Earth Independent

Orion spacecraft missions to Mars

In-space habitat / Mars transfer spacecraft

Earth

Mars

SECOND
SIGHT

The Argus II is an implant designed to restore some sensation of sight to visually-impaired people. In a healthy eye, the lens focuses light on to the retina at the back of the eyeball, which in turn converts the light into electrical signals that the brain decodes as images. Reduced sight or even blindness can occur if the retina is damaged. The Argus II seeks to compensate for this non-functioning part of the eye.

Retina implant

A grid of electrodes is surgically implanted inside the eye, which stimulates the retina. A wireless link connects the electrodes to the rest of the Argus II system outside the user's body.

Inside the eye

A tiny camera captures the view ahead.

A video unit relays image data to an antenna.

A radio antenna links the external equipment with an implant inside the eye.

The Argus II

The Argus II has two parts – one outside the body and the other inside. The external part looks like a pair of dark glasses connected to a small computer. The other part is a tiny electronics package implanted in the eye.

The video processing unit is connected to the glasses by a cable.

Personal medicine

Your DNA contains your unique genetic code, which tells every part of your body what to do. In the future, it's possible that DNA could be used to treat illnesses, with doctors analysing code and prescribing medicine that is tailored to treat the unique genetic profile of their patients.

A strand of DNA

HOW IT WORKS

1 A tiny camera mounted in the middle of the eye-glasses captures the scene in front of the wearer and converts it into an electrical signal. This is sent to the video processing unit (VPU), which prepares it for the implant.

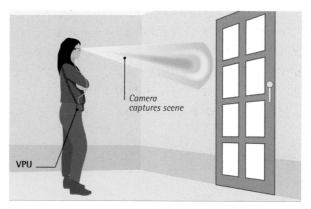

Camera captures scene

VPU

2 The processed video signal is sent to a radio transmitter antenna mounted on the side of the glasses. The transmitted signal is picked up by a receiver attached to the eye and relayed to the implant inside the eye.

Electronics case

Implant

Antenna

3 The processed video signal is sent to a grid of 60 electrodes inside the eye. The electrodes stimulate the retina's remaining working cells. They pass the signal down the optic nerve to the brain, which enables you to see spots of light.

Image is flipped by the eye to "see" the door shape

Retina

Electrodes stimulate the retina with visual patterns that the user learns to read

HOW IT WORKS

⩓ A V-shaped array of long floating barriers will catch plastic waste. These barriers don't need to move to collect the plastic. In fact, they are anchored to the ocean floor. Nature will do the work. The barriers will be placed in locations where ocean currents will carry the plastic towards them.

Waste collects here.

Floating barriers trap waste

⩓ Not all of the plastic waste in the ocean floats. Some of it is suspended below the surface. Screens hanging down under the booms will gather this subsurface waste. Most of the water current will pass under these screens. Fish and other sea creatures will also be able to swim under the screens.

Subsurface barrier

Screens trap subsurface waste

⩓ The V shape of the barriers is the key to their operation. Once waste is trapped behind a barrier, ocean currents will move it towards the point of the V, where a central platform will extract the waste. It will then be stored on-site until it can be transported to land for recycling or disposal.

Boom

Waste extraction and storage

THE OCEAN CLEANUP PROJECT

Every year, millions of tonnes of plastic waste enters the world's oceans. Ultraviolet radiation breaks it down into smaller and smaller pieces by a process called photodegradation. This plastic waste isn't just unsightly, it's dangerous. The chemicals it contains harm the creatures that eat the plastic. The Ocean Cleanup project aims to collect this waste and remove it from the oceans by using specially designed floating barriers.

⟫ Testing floating barriers

The Ocean Cleanup's barriers have been tested in the North Sea, collecting balls instead of rubbish. The next step is to test them in the ocean. A 2,000-m (6,562-ft) long barrier will be installed in the Tsushima Strait off the coast of Japan in 2016.

Wind and currents carry plastic towards a floating barrier.

Prevention

While the Ocean Cleanup project removes plastic waste already in the ocean, it's important to prevent more plastic getting into the ocean in the first place. A lot of it is washed down rivers from cities. Floating booms similar to Ocean Cleanup's barriers are already being used in some river mouths to trap rubbish.

Plastic pollution

The five ocean gyres

Great Pacific Garbage Patch **01**

Indian Ocean Gyre **02**

South Pacific Gyre **03**

North Atlantic Gyre **05**

South Atlantic Gyre **04**

Ocean gyres

The ocean currents that concentrate plastic waste at sea are called gyres. There are five of them. They flow round and round in circles, trapping floating waste in the middle. A third of all the plastic in the oceans is trapped in the biggest gyre. It's called the Great Pacific Garbage Patch and it's located in the North Pacific Gyre between the west coast of the United States and Japan. About 80 per cent of the debris it contains came from land, and the rest was dumped by ships.

A platform extracts the plastic and stores it for collection and removal.

Plastic debris builds up behind the barrier.

LIVING IN THE ISS

The International Space Station (ISS) is a space laboratory that was assembled, bit-by-bit, 400 km (250 miles) above the surface of Earth. It has been continuously occupied since 2000, and in that time, more than 200 astronauts from 15 countries have worked in its weightless environment. These astronauts conduct research to advance our understanding of science – from how humans can live in space to how to prepare for exploration beyond Earth.

The giant in space

The ISS is the biggest and costliest structure ever built in space. It's the size of a football field and its cost is estimated at around $100 billion. On Earth, it would weigh 420,000 kg (930,000 lb). It is powered by electricity generated by 2,500 m² (27,000 ft²) of solar panels.

ISS in orbit around Earth

Robot arms attached to the space station move equipment and supplies around.

The Harmony module houses power gear and has six ports for linking other modules.

Life on board

❧ The space station needs regular maintenance work and occasional repairs. Sometimes, astronauts have to don spacesuits and go outside to do this work. ISS astronauts have made about 200 spacewalks.

❧ Daily exercise is vital to maintain the crew's health and fitness, and stave off the effects of weightlessness. The astronauts use an exercise bike and treadmill to help minimize the loss of muscle and bone.

❧ ISS astronauts carry out experiments in a variety of physical and biological sciences, including studies of plant growth. This is important because future astronauts will have to grow their own food.

❧ When the astronauts aren't working, they relax by reading, listening to music, and watching films. They also like to spend time watching Earth through the Cupola's windows, the largest fitted to any spacecraft.

The Japanese Kibo module is a science laboratory where astronauts work.

Docking ports enable spacecraft to link up with the space station.

The Cupola's seven windows are used for making observations of Earth.

⬆ Working in orbit

Astronauts spend about 35 hours each week conducting research and experiments in the spacecraft's weightless environment. The station travels at a speed of 7.6 km (5 miles) a second, and completes an orbit of Earth every 90 minutes.

MEDICAL MARVELS

Medical science tends to be at the forefront of technology as small advances can help to cure disease and save lives. The miniaturization of electronics means that computing devices may soon be working on or inside your body, and technology that takes control of the way a body grows will be able to replace body parts completely.

Biostamp tattoo

In future, doctors might use biostamps to monitor a patient's health. The temporary tattoo is an ultra-thin microchip that is waterproof and able to move with the skin. The chip will send data on things like activity levels, hydration, and blood pressure via a wireless transmitter, giving doctors a better picture of how the patient's body is working over a couple of weeks.

Anti-virus robots

DNA carries our genetic code in a precise sequence of chemical units. If a virus or illness invades the body, future biomedical engineers may be able to program new, non-genetic DNA molecules to be delivered to the affected parts of the body by tiny robots. The robots deliver their load and fix the problem, before decaying into harmless fragments.

Synthetic skin

A flexible plastic laced with silicon and gold is being developed as a touch-sensitive, synthetic skin. Tiny electronic sensors inside it can pick up pressure, heat, cold, and moisture, thus offering the same span of senses as human skin.

Organ growing

Researchers have learned how to grow extra kidneys inside lab rats, a process that could be scaled up to make it possible to grow new organs inside human bodies to replace damaged ones. The system requires special human body cells to be grown in the lab. These are then implanted into an adult body, where they continue to grow into a new organ.

Model patient

SimMan is a robot patient used to teach nurses and doctors how to look after real people. Trainers can instruct it to speak, bleed, sweat, breathe in and out, go to the toilet, and even cry. The robot can simulate the many different ways human patients need help from medical staff, giving them a valuable chance to practise, without harming anyone if they get it wrong.

6 FUTURE

Some of the inventions in this chapter haven't been created yet. They are possible in theory – we just need to figure out how to make them work. Other concepts have already been realized. Artificial intelligence is already pretty sophisticated, and commuter drones are not science fiction, but do exist. We will have to wait a little longer for flying cars, quantum computers, and teleportation machines. The future will be full of the coolest stuff imaginable.

≫ Modular phone

Phonebloks is the brainchild of Dutch designer Dave Hakkens. The phone is fully customizable – meaning each user can have a phone that suits his or her personal preferences and needs – it's as easy as selecting the parts.

Plug-in modules on the back give the phone its suite of features and capabilities.

HOW IT WORKS

Phonebloks modules plug into a base, or motherboard. This connects the modules so they communicate with one another. Two screws lock everything together. Users choose modules to suit their needs. For example, they might choose a basic phone camera or a more sophisticated camera module made by a camera manufacturer.

Users create their own phone with the specific set of features they want.

A bigger battery could be chosen by someone who might go longer without being able to charge their phone than most.

Standard-sized, interchangeable modules fit every phone.

Modules have metal pins that plug into holes in the base.

PHONEBLOKS

One of the most visible pieces of technology in our modern world is the mobile phone. But with most people changing their phone regularly to keep up with the latest technology, the disposal of old phones has created mountains of waste. A concept called Phonebloks seeks to reduce this waste by creating a phone made of separate pieces called modules that can be easily replaced.

A replaceable touchscreen covers the front of the phone and displays the available features.

The parts

There are plug-in modules for every part of the phone. They include touchscreen, camera, Wi-Fi, battery, memory, speaker, Bluetooth, microphone, power supply, ringer, and gyroscope modules.

Electronic waste

Hundreds of millions of mobile phones are thrown away every year. They contain valuable materials that can be recovered. A million mobile phones contain 34 kg (75 lb) of gold, 350 kg (770 lb) of silver, 15 kg (30 lb) of palladium, and 16,000 kg (35,000 lb) of copper. Taiwanese artist Lin Shih-Pao built a car from 25,000 used mobile phones to show how they can be recycled as art.

Lin Shih-Pao's installation

PASSENGER
DRONE

Drones are uncrewed aircraft piloted by remote control or flying autonomously. The Ehang 184 is a drone with a difference – human cargo. This octocopter – so named for its eight independent rotors – has no pilot. Its passenger selects a flight plan and destination, and the drone does the rest, able to carry a person on a 20-minute flight at speeds of up to 100 kph (62 mph).

Droneport

It is estimated that only one-third of Africans live within walking distance of an all-season road, which means that getting vital medical supplies to isolated communities is a huge problem. Rwanda, dubbed the "land of a thousand hills", has been selected as the location of the world's first droneport. It is hoped that automated long-distance drones, taking off from the droneport, will be able to go where roads don't, and take life-saving supplies to some of the most remote areas on Earth.

A droneport concept for Rwanda

The drone is made from moulded carbon-fibre and lightweight aluminium.

The rotors work in pairs, with each one spinning in the opposite direction to its partner.

The drone's flight lights are suited to day and night flying.

« Safety first

The battery-powered Ehang 184 is a fully automated drone with room for one passenger. Designed with safety in mind, it has eight rotors and eight independent power supplies, which ensure the aircraft will always be able to fly, even if one fails.

HOW IT WORKS

A tablet in the passenger cabin controls the Ehang's flight plan. This connects with a central server, which coordinates the journey with other aircraft in the area, overriding flight requests when flight conditions are poor. The drone follows an inverted U flight path, taking off and landing vertically and cruising at a constant altitude of 500 m (1,640 ft), using satellite data to navigate its flight path.

The passenger can check the status of the aircraft and control cabin conditions.

A live GPS map shows the drone's progress during the flight.

The passenger can decide to hover or land at any location.

The drone control app runs on a normal tablet computer

BECOMING
INVISIBLE

Most people have probably wondered what it might be like to be invisible, but there is currently no way of making people disappear. That may not be the case for much longer, however, as some scientists are trying to develop ways to make things invisible, and they've had some success. So far, these prototype invisibility systems work only under strictly controlled laboratory conditions, and for relatively small things. The next step is to take them out of the laboratory and make them work in the real world. If they are successful, you might be flitting by unseen before you know it!

What use is invisibility?

» The ability to make someone or something invisible is interesting, but what use would it be? Imagine the view from an airliner with an invisible floor or walls. People who study wild animals and film them usually have to hide from view. Their work would be a lot easier if they could make themselves invisible.

African lioness in her natural habitat

B-2 Bomber

« Military forces are very interested in invisibility research. Stealth technology has rendered aircraft such as the B-2 stealth bomber virtually undetectable by radar. Imagine how much more difficult it would be to fight against soldiers, tanks, or aircraft if they could be made more difficult to see or even invisible on the battlefield.

The disappearing hand trick

Researchers at the University of Rochester in New York, USA, have succeeded in making things vanish. Unlike other invisibility systems, which rely on complex arrangements of cameras and mirrors, the Rochester system uses inexpensive lenses.

Lenses bend light around the hand.

Part of the hand vanishes, but the background remains visible.

HOW IT WORKS

The University of Rochester's invisibility system relies on the ability of lenses to bend light. One lens concentrates a background image into a narrow beam. Two more lenses stop the beam from expanding until it reaches the fourth lens, which restores the image to its original size. Anything placed outside the narrow beam (the cloaked region) will not be seen through the fourth lens.

5 The final lens expands the light beam, reproducing the pattern over the hand.

1 Light from the pattern enters the first lens.

2 The first lens produces a narrow light beam.

3 Extra lenses keep the beam narrow.

Anything outside the narrow beam becomes invisible.

4 The light beam passes between the splayed fingers.

SPACE FRONTIERS

The new rockets and spacecraft that will be needed to help us explore further in space are already being built and tested. Engineers are also thinking about how to do things that seem impossible today. It is possible that faster-than-light galactic travel, elevators reaching to space, and hibernating astronauts will all become reality.

SLS

The US space agency NASA is developing the world's most powerful rocket for launching craft carrying astronauts and cargo into orbit. Called the Space Launch System (SLS), its first flight is scheduled for 2021. SLS will be able to lift 130 tonnes – more than the weight of 85 family cars – and take people further into space than ever before.

Space tether

An unusual idea for moving spacecraft in space is to use a long cable known as a space tether. As a spacecraft passes through a planet's magnetic field, electricity flows along the tether. The energy could perhaps be channelled as a fuel-saving power. A rotating tether might also be used to catch a spacecraft and catapult it into a higher orbit.

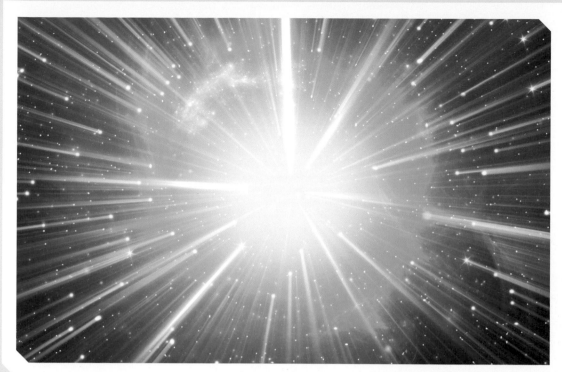

Warp drive

To travel faster than light, starships in films are said to have the ability to expand the space behind them and contract the space in front of them. Scientifically speaking, the idea could potentially work, but we currently do not have the ability to do it. If we could find a way, it would allow us to venture further in our Universe than we could even imagine now.

Space lift

Imagine riding a lift from Earth into space. Engineers suggest that such a creation could be made of super-strong carbon ribbons, anchored to the ground and extending 100,000 km (62,000 miles) into space. Elevator cars would climb up the ribbons into space.

Sleeper craft

For long space flights to Mars and beyond, NASA is investigating the possibility of putting astronauts into a deep sleep called torpor, similar to hibernation in animals. This might be done by lowering the astronauts' body temperature. They could then be woken on arrival.

HYPERLOOP

Imagine taking a trip at speeds of 1,220 kph (760 mph). You could go from San Francisco to Los Angeles in the USA – a journey that normally takes nearly six hours by road – in only 30 minutes. The extraordinary vehicle that could make this possible is called the Hyperloop. Passengers will sit in capsules inside a tube that serves as the track. A combination of magnets, electricity, and air causes the capsule to zip by. Each section of the tube is flexible, meaning it is earthquake-proof, and the capsules are prevented from bumping into one another by air pressure.

HOW IT WORKS

A Hyperloop capsule will be propelled by electromagnetic motors. When an electric current is applied, magnets in the capsule and track cause the capsule to move forwards. A fan sucks in air from the front of the capsule, and blows most of it backwards behind it. Some of it is blown downwards to create a cushion that supports the capsule instead of wheels, like a puck on an air hockey table.

Inside the nose cone, a fan sucks in air and pushes it backwards and downwards.

Each passenger cabin is big enough for 6–8 people.

Magnetic forces boost the Hyperloop's speed or slow it down.

The Hyperloop's streamlined body slips through the remaining air in the tunnel easily.

Comparing speeds

Hyperloop aims to combine the speed of air transport, or even faster speeds, with the convenience of rail travel. Its average speed would be about 965 kph (600 mph) – a little faster than an airliner's cruising speed. At this speed, it would be three times faster than a Japanese bullet train and it would easily win a race against the current rail speed record holder in passenger service, the Shanghai Maglev Train (SMT).

Hyperloop
1,220 kph (760 mph)

Commercial airliner
900 kph (560 mph)

Maglev train
430 kph (270 mph)

Bullet train
300 kph (185 mph)

Top speed

∨ Super fast travel

Hyperloop will whisk passengers from city to city faster than a jet airliner. You may not be able to enjoy the view, though, because the capsules will travel inside tubes. Test tracks are being built to develop the concept's technology.

Most of the air is sucked out of the tunnel to enable the capsule to travel faster.

Hyperloop has no wheels. Instead, it rides on top of a thin cushion of air.

HOW IT WORKS

1 A traveller stands in a teleporter pod, which scans the traveller and maps the positions of all the matter in his body.

2 Powerful scanning disrupts the atoms in the traveller's body and causes the person to dematerialize.

3 The scan data is transmitted. It is received by another pod, which uses it to recreate, or materialize, the traveller.

⟫ Arriving safely

Teleportation is not so much travelling as communication between two points – only the message in this case is your whole body. The possibility of being able to go on holiday in seconds is a long way off, but may be possible.

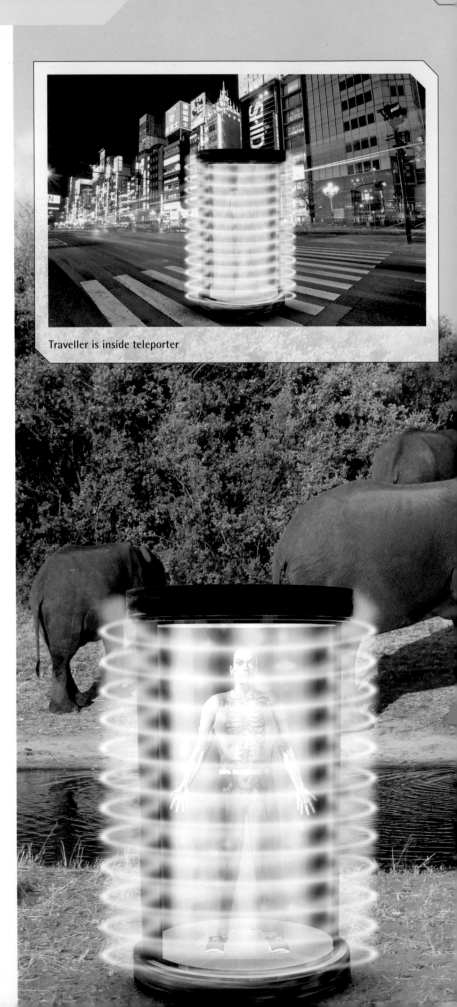

Traveller is inside teleporter

TELEPORTATION

What would it be like to dematerialize in a teleporter? Would your thoughts, memories, and personality be teleported, along with the particles that make up your body? Would the teleported person really be "you" in every way? This may seem impossible, but some scientists are actually carrying out research and experimentation in teleportation and they've had some success. So far, only a tiny bit of light energy has been teleported this way, with a record distance currently of 143 km (89 miles). It might not be impossible after all!

Quantum leap

Quantum entanglement

⌃ Teleportation research uses something called quantum entanglement. Two particles or photons are entangled if they are synchronized so closely that altering one automatically alters the other, even if they are far apart. It enables scientists to teleport bits of quantum information (called qubits) in experiments.

Teleportation may improve credit card security

⌃ Long before it becomes possible to teleport people (if it ever does), quantum teleportation could lead to lightning-fast Internet services and better credit card security because they all involve moving a lot of information quickly.

INTERNET OF
THINGS

There are more devices connected to the Internet than there are people on Earth. As this number increases, and the devices become interconnected, it will form the Internet of Things (IoT). The IoT will give people remote access to their house and office and allow them to interact in new ways with public spaces such as shops, tourist attractions, and transport networks. The data collected by these devices will be used to build intelligent systems that help people live healthier and more efficient lives.

The oven can be controlled remotely or follow instructions from a recipe to come on at the right temperature and at the right time for each day's meals.

Lights come on automatically as a person approaches a room, using signals from his or her personal activity tracker. The lighting level adapts to the time of day and weather, and responds to activity such as eating, watching TV, or working.

A chip on your pet monitors its activity and location, giving a warning if it enters forbidden areas, and opening feeders when it is hungry.

Biometric locks on the exterior doors record who is currently in the house, and can be programmed to open to accept pre-arranged deliveries.

Weather forecasts and sensors around the house are used to adjust the temperature inside the home to keep it at optimal levels for the time of day and the homeowner's preference.

The refrigerator scans food to track what items are inside, how long they have been there, how often they are used, and how much is left.

As well as being used for watching television, the screens in the house are controllers for all the other systems in the home.

HOW IT WORKS

In the home, the IoT will work by coordinating smart devices, and analysing the behaviour of their owner. This means that one system, such as a smart fridge, can learn to manage a person's groceries automatically, taking into consideration the habits of the owner. It can also attempt to improve the owner's health by suggesting solutions to simple problems, such as ordering healthier food for the refrigerator, or diagnosing an illness.

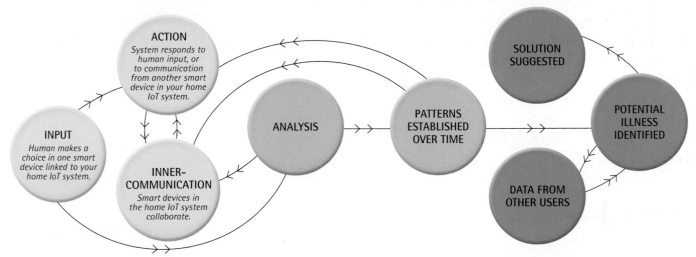

ACTION
System responds to human input, or to communication from another smart device in your home IoT system.

INPUT
Human makes a choice in one smart device linked to your home IoT system.

INNER-COMMUNICATION
Smart devices in the home IoT system collaborate.

ANALYSIS

PATTERNS ESTABLISHED OVER TIME

SOLUTION SUGGESTED

POTENTIAL ILLNESS IDENTIFIED

DATA FROM OTHER USERS

≈ When a human inputs something into one smart device of their home IoT system, the action occurs, but it will also result in adjustments to other parts of the system – for instance if you turn the TV on, the lights will dim.

≈ Human inputs are analysed and patterns established. For example, if you normally watch TV on Tuesday nights, the TV and the lights will learn this: the TV will turn on and the lights will automatically dim on Tuesday nights if you are there.

≈ Your IoT system can take information from various smart devices to fix problems you might be unaware of. It could take information from your activity tracker, fridge, and even your toilet to tell if you are ill, and then use data from other people to suggest a solution for you.

≪ Internet at home

The Internet of Things will transform the home, connecting everyday devices together. They can all be operated remotely from central controllers, but these systems also share information and respond automatically to each other's actions.

Traffic congestion

On the road

Outside of our everyday lives, the IoT will revolutionize your everyday life in interesting ways. Traffic jams may be a thing of the past as the IoT takes up-to-the-minute information from all modes of transport to keep you on the move. This data will then present you with the best routes around delays, but the IoT will not send everybody the same route, reducing the chances of further jams on alternative routes.

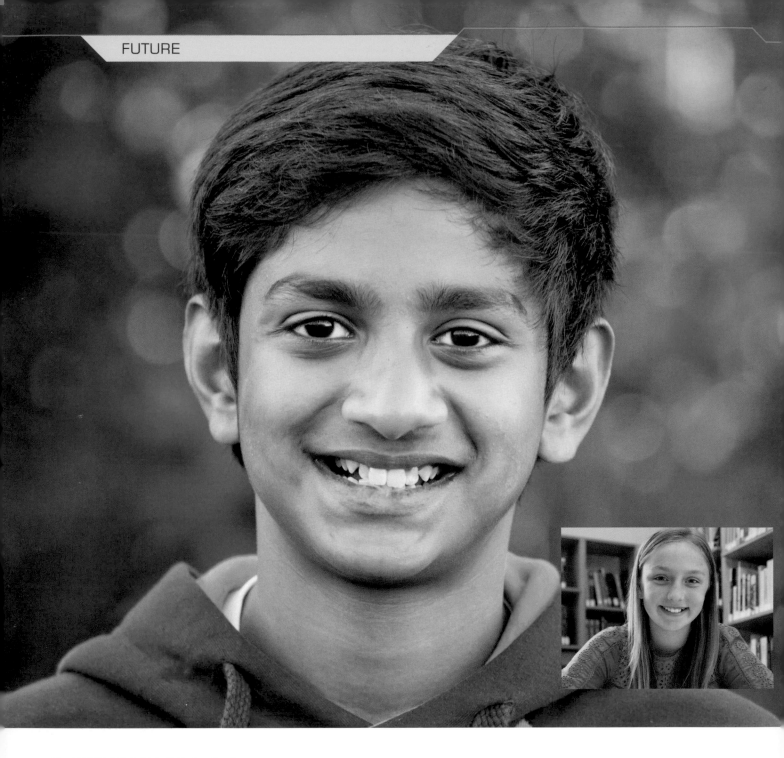

ARTIFICIAL
INTELLIGENCE

Computers are getting better at acting like humans. As a result, artificial intelligence (AI) is progressing at an unprecedented rate, and often in areas you might not realize. AI systems are now able to diagnose diseases from a set of symptoms, play complex board games against human competitors, and translate speech from one language to another in real time. As an AI does these things and more, it learns from the things that happen afterwards, much in the way that humans do – with each situation improving the AI system's understanding of future situations.

नमस्ते मेरा नाम किंषुक है। आप कैसी हैं?

Hello, my name is Kingshuk. How are you?

Hello Kingshuk, I'm Smiljka. I'm in school — we are having a lesson about India. Where in the country do you live?

नमस्ते किंषुक। मेरा नाम स्मीका है। मैं स्कूल में हूँ। हम लोग इंडिया के बारे मे पढ़ रहे हैं। आप इंडिया में कहाँ रहते हैं?

मैं नई दिल्ली में रहता हूँ। मुझे यह जगह बहुत पसंद है। यह एक ऐतिहासिक शहर है और यहाँ का खाना काफ़ी स्वादिष्ट है। आप कहाँ रहती हैं?

I live in New Delhi — I really love it. This is a historic city and the food here is delicious. Where do you live?

I live near London. It's nice but it's very cold right now.

मैं लंदन के पास रहती हूँ। यह जगह अच्छी है मगर इस समय यहाँ बहुत सर्दी है।

Type a message in English here

≪ Breaking language barriers

Skype Translator is one example of an AI system. It enables people speaking in two different languages to have a conversation in real time. The translator recognizes what is said in one language and translates it into another, and back again.

HOW IT WORKS

AI-driven translators, such as Skype Translator, enable you to talk to your friends in real time, even if they do not speak the same language as you. The artificial intelligence at work here is the translator's ability to understand exactly what the speakers mean, which is determined by the translator breaking down the noises you make into small parts, and comparing them with known words in its Internet-linked database. It must be able to do this in a split second in order for a conversation to run smoothly.

1 When the first person speaks, the translator analyses the sound and compares it to recorded audio snippets in its database to identify the words.

It's ah nice but it's very cold right now.

"it's ah nice..."
"it's ah nice..."
"it's nice..."

2 Any unnecessary sounds – such as "ums", "ahs", and repetitions – are removed from the speech as they are unimportant to its meaning.

3 Skype Translator then uses its artificially intelligent "knowledge" of languages to translate the words into the second person's language.

ENGLISH
HINDI

यह जगह अच्छी है मगर इस समय यहाँ बहुत सर्दी है।

4 The translated words are shown to the second person, and can be spoken by the program's voice generator. A response from the second person starts the cycle again.

Con...

The D...
this s...
vacuu...
proce...
powe...
the c...
consi...

The Turing Test

In 1950, the English mathematician Alan Turing developed a test to check whether or not a machine is intelligent. The test, which became known as the Turing Test, involves a person and a machine communicating with each other using text. If the person can't tell whether he or she is communicating with a machine or another person, then the machine has passed the test.

The D...

WHAT'S NEXT?

TRANSPORT

Transport will probably develop in three ways: super-fast vehicles for carrying people who can't wait, more spacious and comfortable transport for the masses, and large robotic cargo vehicles for hauling goods all around the world.

» Electric and hydrogen-fuelled vehicles will become more popular than vehicles running on fossil fuels.

» Self-driving cars and trucks will make road transport safer.
» Airliners using the latest scientific research will jet people around the globe faster than the speed of sound.
» Hypersonic (more than five times faster than the speed of sound) aircraft will make it possible to fly halfway round the world in only a couple of hours.

MILITARY

The Internet, GPS, radar, jet engines, and computers all had their origins in military research, and the military will continue to be a major driver of innovation and invention.

» Unmanned Combat Air Vehicles (UCAVs) will replace manned attack planes and autonomous robots, and remotely controlled vehicles will become commonplace.
» Stealth technology and conventional camouflage will be enhanced by increasingly effective invisibility systems.
» Governments around the world will spend more time and money on securing their countries against attacks on their national security from the Internet.

SPACE

Following the first manned landing on Mars in the 2030s, space agencies begin to plan for their next manned landing – possibly on one of Jupiter's moons. Meanwhile, private companies will continue to exploit near-Earth space.

» The first privately funded space station will receive its first guests for a holiday in orbit.
» A new Space Race to establish the first permanently manned Moonbase will be contested between the United States and China.
» A space probe will land on Jupiter's moon Europa and bore down through the surface ice into the ocean below to search for life.
» Space telescopes may observe a planet that appears to exhibit signs of intelligent life, including radio transmissions, and a debris field that may be the remains of rockets and spacecraft.
» Scientists may begin transforming Mars to prepare for the day when human settlers start moving there.

COMMUNICATIONS

Communications encompass everything from newspapers and broadcasting to broadband and telephones – and all will be transformed by future technologies.

» Smartphones will not remain as stand-alone handsets for much longer, but are likely to be built into all sorts of other devices.
» Traditional news organizations will cease to exist, and be replaced by individuals posting reports, eyewitness accounts, and opinions pieces online on their own video channels.
» In a few decades, personal computers will be as powerful as today's supercomputers.
» Television will be broadcast in UDTV (Ultra-high Definition TV), with 16 times the definition of television today.

ENERGY

Increasing global energy demands will drive improvements in existing sources of energy and the development of new energy sources. Environmental concerns mean that new energy technologies will have to be clean and green.

» After decades of research, the first nuclear power stations based on atomic fusion will be built.
» Airborne wind turbines tethered to the ground will generate electricity from high-speed, high-altitude winds.
» Countries with access to the sea will extract hydrogen from sea water and use it as a fuel for electricity generation and transport.
» Solar power satellites may be launched to capture solar energy and beam it down to Earth.

BIOTECHNOLOGY

Biotechnology, the combination of living organisms and technology to solve problems and make commercial products, is expected to have a far-reaching impact on four fields in particular: medicine, agriculture, industry, and the environment.

》 Genetically improved photosynthesis will increase crop yields to help feed the growing global population.
》 Sensors built from genetically engineered living cells will be implanted in the human body to collect medical data.
》 Solar panels will be grown from living plant cells.
》 Super-fast computer memory devices will be made from naturally magnetic bacteria.
》 Bacteria will be employed to clean up pollution.

NANOTECHNOLOGY

Tiny technologies will find applications throughout all sorts of industries, including manufacturing, agriculture, electronics, energy, and healthcare. Materials created to order, atom by atom, will be tailored to the precise properties needed for each application.

》 Nanotech coatings on buildings and bridges will neutralize air pollution.
》 Diamond-like materials 50 times stronger than steel will be developed by nanotechnology.
》 Nanobots the size of blood cells will be injected into the human body to repair damage, or seek out invaders such as viruses, bacteria, and cancer cells.
》 Taking nanotechnology even further to smaller scales called picotechnology and femtotechnology will be used to manipulate matter at the atomic and subatomic scale.

ROBOTICS

Robots will become an increasingly common feature of our lives. More capable, Internet-linked robots with more advanced artificial intelligence will work alongside human workers in business and industry. Labour-saving robotic devices will become more common in our homes.

》 As artificial intelligence improves, robots will be able to do an increasing number of jobs, and potentially do them better than humans.
》 Japan, the world leader in robot technology, will send humanoid robots into space in place of astronauts.
》 Robots will begin to replace dogs to guide blind people and assist people with other disabilities.

EVERYDAY LIFE

Technology will continue to subtly affect our everyday lives, with many small advances such as faster Internet connections making new ways of working and learning possible.

» Schools may be phased out in favour of live streaming of lessons to children's homes.
» Car manufacturers will produce cars with a self-repairing coating on their bodywork.
» Internet and real-time translation programs will make it possible for people to communicate with each other, in any language, all over the world.
» Coins and banknotes will finally disappear, replaced by digital payment methods.

HEALTH AND MEDICINE

Advances in genetics and biotechnology may finally reveal mechanisms for curing cancer and Alzheimer's Disease, and for repairing damage to spinal cords, eyes, and brains. The cell damage that causes the effects of ageing may be reversible, too.

» It will become possible to upload a human mind to a supercomputer.
» The Internet of DNA may become a reality, enabling researchers to access the genomes of thousands of people online, to increase their ability to find cures for common illnesses.
» New body parts and even whole organs will be made by 3-D bio-printing, printing layer upon layer of living cells.
» Survival rates for many cancers will reach almost 100 per cent, thanks to advances in medical knowledge made possible by technology.
» The cost of expensive drugs will fall when they are mass-produced using genetically engineered organisms instead of making them chemically.

ACKNOWLEDGMENTS

The publisher would like to thank the following people for their help with making the book:
Victoria Pyke for proofreading; Carron Brown for the index; Meenal Goel, Rashika Kachroo, Roshni Kapur for design assistance; Ann Baggaley, Kathakali Banerjee, Shatarupa Chaudhuri, Virien Chopra, Agnibesh Das, Sarah Isle, Sukriti Kapoor, Priyanka Kharbanda, Ashwin Khurana, Deeksha Miglani, and Sonia Yooshing for editorial assistance.

All technologies, names, and designs are protected by copyright and trademark.

Special thanks to all of the manufacturers, design and architectural studios, and photographers who answered numerous queries and gave permission to use their images throughout the book.

Picture Credits
The publisher would like to thank the following for their kind permission to reproduce their photographs:

(Key: a-above, b-below, c-centre, l-left, r-right, t-top)

2 123RF.com: Sebastian Kaulitzki (br). **Artiphon, Inc.** (tl). **Courtesy of Whill:** (bc). **EHANG, Inc.:** (tc). **Getty Images:** Lionel Flusin (ca); Image By Steve Passlow (crb). **Gewers Pudewill:** (clb). **Omer Hacıomeroglu** (cb). **2-191** iStockphoto.com: fazon1 (Background). **4** reactable.com: (cra). **5 Getty Images:** Joseph Viker: (cra). **Rolls-Royce plc:** (cla). **6 Courtesy of D*Haus:** (cra). **Getty Images:** Lionel Flusin (cla). **7 Courtesy of International Business Machines Corporation:** (cla). Terrafugia/www.terrafugia.com: (cra). **8 SHARP corporation:** (bl). **Courtesy of Osmo:** (br). Used with permission from Microsoft: (tl). **ROLI.com:** (cr). **10-11** Used with permission from Microsoft. **10** Used with permission from Microsoft: (cl, bl). **11 U.S. Air Force:** Airman 1st Class Anthony Jennings (bc). **12-13 Samuel Twist. 12 LSST Corporation:** Todd Mason, Mason Productions Inc. (clb). **Rex by Shutterstock:** KeystoneUSA-ZUMA (tl). **13 Courtesy of Gopro:** (br, ca, tl, tr). **14-15** Used with permission from Microsoft: (tc). **14** Used with permission from Microsoft: (br). **15** Used with permission from Microsoft: (cla, br). **16-17** Amazon.com, Inc.: (clb). **17** Amazon.com, Inc.: (br). iStockphoto.com: ZernLiew (cra, tr). **18-19** 3Doodler. **19** Bocusini by Print2Taste: (br). **20** 3Dvarius: Laurent Bernadac (br); Thomas Tetu (bl). **ROLI.com:** (cr). **21 Doppler Labs:** (tc, tl). reactable.com: (b). **Yamaha Music Europe GmbH (UK), Pro Music Department:** (tr). **22-23 Samsung Electronics:** (c). **22 Dreamstime.com:** Guruxox (ca, tc). **Getty Images:** Yoshikazu Tsuno (tl). **Samsung Electronics:** (tr). **24-25 IHS Technology. 25** © 2016 Hello Games Limited: No Man's Sky is a trade mark of Hello Games Limited (tr). **IHS Technology:** (br). **Sony Computer Entertainment UK Limited:** (crb). **26-27 LG Electronics. Corbis:** Fotofeeling / Westend61 (waterfall). **27** 123RF.com: Mariusz Blach (c). **Getty Images:** Jung Yeon-Je (br). **28-29 Artiphon, Inc.:** (All images). **29 Artiphon, Inc.:** (cla). **Getty Images:** Sovfoto (br). Noisy Jelly: (cra). **30-31 Getty Images:** Andrzej Wojcicki / Science Photo Library. **31 NASA:** Emmett Given (br). **32-33 Corbis:** Albert Pena / Icon Sportswire. **32 Dreamstime.com:** Norgal (bl). **34 elemental path:** CogniToys Dino (tr). **Mattel, Inc.:** © 2016 Mattel, Inc. All Rights Reserved (bc). **35 Courtesy of Osmo:** (b). **Wondernik:** (cla, cra). **36-37** Used with permission from Microsoft: (All images). **37 Alamy Stock Photo:** Interfoto (bc). **Science Photo Library:** Manfred Kage (crb). **38-39 Getty Images:** Image By Steve Passlow. **39 Alamy Stock Photo:** Stocktrek Images, Inc. (bc). **40 Jetman Dubai:** (clb). **Hybrid Air Vehicles Ltd.:** (br). **Volocopter: e-volo GmbH** (tl). **ElliptiGO Inc.:** (tr). **42-43 Courtesy of Lexus Division (UK). 42 Lexus:** (cl) **43 Alamy Stock Photo:** Henry Westheim Photography (cr); Stan Rohrer (crb). **Lexus:** (clb). **44-45 SpaceX. 44** Nick Kaloterakis: (clb). **45 Blue Origin:** (cra). **46-47 46 Courtesy of Whill:** (cl). **Courtesy of**

Scalevo: (cla). **47 Courtesy of Whill:** (br, cr, cra). **48-49 Tesla Motors:** (All images). **50-51 Courtesy Virgin Galactic. 51 Corbis:** Sergei Chirikov / epa (crb). **52-53 Wessex Water/ Julian James photography. 52 Amager Resource Center:** (clb). **Science Photo Library:** Pascal Goetgheluck (cl). **54-55 ElliptiGO Inc.. 55 Reuters:** Baz Ratner (cr). **56-57 NASA:** Robert Markowitz. **56 NASA:** MSFC (bl). **57 ESA:** NASA (ca). **NASA:** (bl, br, crb). **58-59 Hybrid Air Vehicles Ltd. 59 Corbis:** John Lund / Blend Images (cla). **60-61 Jetman Dubai:** jetman.com (All images). **62 Courtesy of Superpedestrian:** Michael D Spencer (tr). **iStockphoto.com:** Joe_Potato (b). **63 DFKI GmbH:** (cra). **Nike:** (br). **Courtesy of WaterCar:** (bl); www.WaterCar.com (clb). **64-65** Olivier Cabaret. **64 Airbus-image exm company:** Hervé Goussé (c). **65 Dreamstime. com:** Travis Fisher (tr). **66-67 Rolls-Royce plc. 66** Used with permission of Royal Caribbean Cruises Ltd.: (cra). **67 Rolls-Royce plc:** (tr). **68-69 NASA:** Goddard Space Flight Center. **69 NASA:** JHUAPL / SwRI (c). **70-71 Volocopter:** e-volo GmbH. **Dreamstime.com:** Phanuwatn (grass). **71 Volocopter:** e-volo GmbH (cr). **72** Joseph Viker: (br). **Alamy Stock Photo:** 68images.com - Axel Schmies (bl). **The Solomon R. Guggenheim Museum, New York:** David Heald © SRGF, NY. (tl). **Getty Images:** Kimberley Coole (tr). **74-75 Alamy Stock Photo:** 68images.com - Axel Schmies. **75 Getty Images:** Chris Jackson (cb). **Rex by Shutterstock:** MC Films (br). **Imre Solt:** (cb). **76-77 Adam Mork Architectural Photography. 77 3XN Architects:** (cla). **Adam Mork Architectural Photography:** (br, cr). **78-79 ICEHOTEL, Jukkasjärvi:** Christopher Hauser. **79 Getty Images:** Jonathan Nackstrand (cr). **ICEHOTEL, Jukkasjärvi:** Paulina Holmgren (crb); Martin Smedsén (cb); Asaf Kliger (bc). **80-81** Joseph Viker. **81 Alamy Stock Photo:** blickwinkel (br). **Foster + Partners:** (cr). **82-83 Alamy Stock Photo:** Photos 12. **82 Corbis:** Yann Arthus-Bertrand (cb). **Alamy Stock Photo:** Agencja Fotograficzna Caro (cb). **83** 123RF.com: lachris77 (cr). **Alamy Stock Photo:** Nina Reistad (br). **Dreamstime.com:** Patricia Hofmeester (tr); Francisco Javier Gil Oreja (crb). **Robert Harding Picture Library:** Christian Reister (cra). **84 Heatherwick Studio Rolling Bridge:** Steve Speller (cra). **National Arboretum, Canberra:** John Gollings (b). **85 Corbis:** Charles Pertwee (bl). **Nextoffice:** Parham Taghioff (br). **SHAU:** Architecture by SHAU Indonesia. Photo: Sanrok Studio (tr, tl). **86 Dreamstime.com:** Ronniechua (bc). **Getty Images:** Barcroft (bl). **87 McDowell+Benedetti (architect), Alan Baxter Associates (structural engineer) and Qualter Hall (M&E designer and contractor):** Timothy Soar (All images). **88-89 Latitude Image:** Nicolas Chorier. **88 Dreamstime. com:** Paul Prescott (clb). **Getty Images:** Kimberley Coole (cla). **90-91 The Solomon R. Guggenheim Museum, New York:** David Heald © SRGF, NY. **90 Alamy Stock Photo:** Russell Kord (c). **Art on Track:** (bc). **The Tate Modern:** © Tate, London 2016 (cb). **92-93 Gewers Pudewill. 92** Gewers Pudewill: (cla). **93** Rendering of + POOL. Design by Family & PlayLab. www. pluspool.org: (br). **94-95 Courtesy of Nakheel. 94 Alexander Heilner:** (cla). **95 NASA:** (cla). **96-97 Corbis:** Catherine Bassetti. **96 Corbis:** Catherine Bassetti (cla). **Washington State Department of Transportation:** (clb). **97 Corbis:** Catherine Bassetti (cra). **98** 123RF.com: Sebastian Kaulitzki (br). **TU Delft:** Renee Mors, Delft University of Technology (cl, clb). **99** Jens Bauer/KIT: (bl). Copyright 2016 **HRL Laboratories:** Dan Little Photography (r). **Wyss Institute at Harvard University:** (cl). **100 Corbis:** Jan Woitas / dpa (br); Patrick Pleul / dpa (tl). **Courtesy of Ekso Bionics:** (bl). **102-103 Tesla Motors:** (All images). **104-105** Ken Richardson Photography. **104** Ken Richardson Photography: (c, clb). **105** Ken Richardson Photography: (cla/eyes). **Corbis:** Jan Woitas / dpa (crb). **106-107** raspberrypi.org: (c). **106 Corbis:** Frank Duenzl / dpa (clb). **107 Hackaball Ltd:** (cra). **Dreamstime.com:** Pavelzhuravlev92 (bc/hand). **raspberrypi. org:** (bc/Pi case). **108-109 Corbis:** Patrick Pleul / dpa. **108 Caterpillar Inc.:** (bl). **110-111 Courtesy of Ekso Bionics. 110** naturepl.com: John Abbott (br). **111 Courtesy of Ekso Bionics:** (bl). **112-113** © CERN: Maximilien Brice. **112**

Science Photo Library: Cern (tc); Claudia Marcelloni, CERN (crb). **Getty Images:** Lionel Flusin (cb). **114 GoSun Stove:** (bl, br). **Volvo Car Uk Ltd:** (c). **115 Columbia University's Engineering School:** Konkuk University, Korea Research Institute of Standards and Science, Seoul National University (cr). **Revolights:** (tl). **Kyuho Song:** (bl, bc). **116-117 Kenedy & Violich Architecture, Ltd. 116 SolarWindow Technologies, Inc.:** (cl). **117 Kenedy & Violich Architecture, Ltd:** (cra, crb). **118-119 Rolls-Royce plc. 119 BAE Systems 2007:** (crb). **Rolls-Royce plc:** (cr). **120-121 Corbis:** Cheng Min / Xinhua Press. **121 Corbis:** Xiao Yijiu / Xinhua Press (cl). **122 Corbis:** KTSDESIGN / Science Photo Library (tr). **Getty Images:** Science Photo Library - SCIEPRO (cr). **Omer Hacıomeroglu:** (br). **NASA:** JPL-Caltech (tl). **124-125 Omer Hacıomeroglu. 124 Omer Hacıomeroglu:** (cl). **125 Courtesy of U.S. Navy:** Mass Communication Specialist Seaman Chelsea Kennedy (bc). **126-127 Courtesy of Cleverpet. 127 WÜF,** getwuf.com: (cra). **128-129 Courtesy of D*Haus. 128 Reuters:** (cl). **130-131 Source: Loon:** (c). **131 Source: Loon:** (tc). **132-133 Science Photo Library:** Steve Gschmeissner. **133 Amazon.com, Inc.:** (br). **134-135 Alamy Stock Photo:** Vladislav Ociacia. **134 Össur UK:** (c). **135 Össur UK:** (cr, br). **136-137** PrecisionHawk. **136 Getty Images:** Cessna Citation Jet / AFP (bc). **PrecisionHawk:** (bl, cb, crb). **138-139** Garmin. **138 EMBR labs:** Niccolo Casas (c). **139** Garmin: (cr). **140-141** Panono. **140 Science Photo Library:** Andy Crump (c). **141 Panono:** (b). **142-143 Foster + Partners. 142 Getty Images:** Stocktrek Images (bl). **NASA:** (clb). **143 NASA:** (cla). **144-145 Second Sight Medical Products. 145** Second Sight Medical Products: (cra). **Corbis:** Science Picture Co. (bc). **Second Sight Medical Products:** (r). **146-147** TheOceanCleanup.com. **146 Getty Images:** Paul Kennedy (br). **148 NASA:** (cb, bc). **150 Corbis:** KTSDESIGN / Science Photo Library (b). **Courtesy of MC10 Inc.:** (tl). **151 Corbis:** VOISIN / PHANIE / phanie / Phanie Sarl (cl). **Getty Images:** Science Photo Library - SCIEPRO (crb). **Seoul National University:** Dae-Hyeong Kim (cla). **152 Courtesy of International Business Machines Corporation:** (tr). **Hyperloop Transportation Technologies:** (tl). **153 Terrafugia/www.terrafugia.com:** (b). **154-155 Phonebloks. 154 Phonebloks:** (tr). **155 Corbis:** Ritchie B. Tongo (br). **156-157 EHANG, Inc.. 156 Foster + Partners:** (bl). **157 EHANG, Inc.:** (bc). **158-159 University of Rochester:** J. Adam Fenster. **158 U.S. Air Force:** Staff Sgt Jeremy M. Wilson (bl). **160 NASA:** (bl). **Science Photo Library:** Martin Marietta Corporation (cr). **161 Dreamstime.com:** Peter Jurik (tl). **NASA:** (bl). **SpaceWorks Enterprises, Inc.:** (crb). **162-163 Hyperloop Transportation Technologies. 164-165 Dreamstime.com:** Brian Sedgbeer. **164 Dorling Kindersley:** Jamie Marshall (cra/Street). **Science Photo Library:** Christian Darkin (cra, br). **165 Corbis:** Hero Images (crb). **Science Photo Library:** Richard Kail (cr). **166** 123RF.com: Valerijs Kostreckis. **168-169 Alamy Stock Photo:** Blend Images (girl); Design Pics Inc (boy). **170-171 Terrafugia/www.terrafugia.com. 170** Terrafugia/www.terrafugia.com: (br). **171 Corbis:** (bc); Ed Darack / Science Faction (br). **172-173 NASA:** Northrop Grumman. **173 NASA:** (cr). **174-175** © D-Wave Systems Inc. All rights reserved. **175 NASA:** Quantum Artificial Intelligence Laboratory (bl). **Courtesy of International Business Machines Corporation:** (bc). **177 NASA:** (crb). **Science Photo Library:** Mark Garlick (cr). **177 Alamy Stock Photo:** Event Horizon Telescope / UPI (bl). **191 Alamy Stock Photo:** Columbia University's Engineering School: Konkuk University, Korea Research Institute of Standards and Science, Seoul National University (tc). **Corbis:** John Lund / Blend Images (tr). **DFKI GmbH:** (bc). **NASA:** Lockheed Martin Corporation (crb). **Science Photo Library:** Claudia Marcelloni, CERN (b). **The Solomon R. Guggenheim Museum, New York:** David Heald © SRGF, NY. (cla). **Courtesy Virgin Galactic:** (ca).

All other images © Dorling Kindersley
For further information see: www.dkimages.com